A Smile for My Parents

A Smile for My Parents

HEATHER HENDERSON

ALLEN&UNWIN
SYDNEY • MELBOURNE • AUCKLAND • LONDON

Published by Allen & Unwin in 2013

Allen & Unwin
83 Alexander Street
Crows Nest NSW 2065
Australia
Phone: (61 2) 8425 0100
Fax: (61 2) 9906 2218
Email: info@allenandunwin.com
Web: www.allenandunwin.com

Cataloguing-in-Publication details are available
from the National Library of Australia
www.trove.nla.gov.au

ISBN 978 1 74331 570 5

Set in 12.25/17.75 pt Granjon by Bookhouse, Sydney
Printed in Australia by McPherson's Printing Group

10 9 8 7 6 5 4 3 2 1

MIX
Paper from responsible sources
FSC
www.fsc.org
FSC® C001695

The paper in this book is FSC® certified. FSC® promotes environmentally responsible, socially beneficial and economically viable management of the world's forests.

For Edwina, Penelope, Catriona, Elizabeth
Better known to us as: Dwina, Penny, Trini, Sibby.
Daughters are the most wonderful invention.

A Smile For My Parents

Adapted from Virgil, *Eclogues*, Book Four.

Contents

Introduction

Years ago, our daughter Edwina told me that I was always saying things about 'Papa' and 'Mama' – my parents – that she hadn't heard before, and would I please write them down. This refrain was taken up by her three sisters and my husband, Peter.

I am well aware that there is considerable interest in Sir Robert and Dame Pattie Menzies, even now. And I'm constantly reminded that many people, particularly some of those who make public comments, have absolutely no idea what my parents were really like.

In 2000 my journalist son-in-law wrote:

> I understand your frustration and disappointment with the article in the paper this week. It is one example of a wider problem. The story you really want to tell must be told directly by you, rather than having it appropriated by someone else.
>
> What that article has done is demonstrate that there IS great interest, still, in the real Bob Menzies, the human side of the political figure – Papa rather than Pig Iron Bob. Only you can tell that story. Get to it.

Even longer ago I received a letter from a 1985 Menzies Scholar, David Morgan. He is now an orthopaedic surgeon and Associate Professor at Queensland University. Following a Menzies Foundation dinner, he wrote:

> I thoroughly enjoyed the stories of your life with Sir Robert. It would be a great pity if these stories were lost. I would urge you to compile them into some form of publication which could be used by The Menzies Foundation and by the Australian public at large.

The Very Reverend Fred McKay, with his wife, Meg, spent many years in central and northern Australia as a Presbyterian minister, where he followed John Flynn as the head of the Australian Inland Mission. He was described by my father as a 'good practical Christian'. He conducted the funeral services of my brother Ian, my father, and my mother. He played a major part in Peter's and my wedding in 1955. He even agreed to marry one of our daughters under the gum trees in the Blue Mountains. In 1992 our daughter Penny wrote to him, 'At my grandfather's funeral I said that if I ever got married I would like you to marry me. Well, now I am getting married, but we want to get married under the gum trees at Blackheath, and maybe you wouldn't like that.' Fred's response was, 'Penny darling, I would marry you under a coolibah tree on the Cooper River.'

So, with a pretty good knowledge of the Menzies family, he wrote to me: 'Meg and I are more and more convinced that you should get cracking on that book of books which you just have to write. "VIL GOD I HAIF".' (This is the motto of the Menzies clan, which is also written as 'Vil God I Zal'. It is translated on our crest as 'Will God I Shall'.) That was in 1999.

Years ago, Tony Abbott told me: 'It is your civic duty.'

Increasingly, I have been invited by various organisations to talk about my parents. A recurring question from my listeners is: 'Have you written this down? Have you written a book?'

I am well aware that many authors struggle to invent characters for their books. I had mine presented to me on a plate. It's just a pity that my talent for procrastination means this is too late for many of the people who knew my parents.

I am grateful to all those who persuaded me to sit down and get on with it.

Family Is Precious

My father's mother, Kate Sampson, was of Cornish descent. Her father was a miner and helped to form the Australian Miners' Union, but her brother, Sydney, was non-Labor and represented Wimmera in the federal parliament for thirteen years. My father's father, James Menzies, was of Scottish descent. He became a shire councillor, then shire president, then the Member for Lowan in the Victorian parliament.

Thus, with both sides of politics represented in the family, politics was well and truly in my father's blood.

My grandfather went to work at the age of sixteen, when his father died. Being artistic, he became a coach painter. As my father wrote in *Afternoon Light*, 'Those were the days when both horse-drawn vehicles and locomotive engines were decorated by pictures of flowers and the like.'

In 1894, with three small children – James Leslie (Les), Frank Gladstone (Frank), and Isabel Alice (Belle) – my grandparents moved from Ballarat to Jeparit, where they opened a small general store. On 20 December that year, their fourth child, my father, Robert Gordon, was born. Sydney Keith (Syd) was born ten years later.

The children had a lot of freedom in the small country town, but at the same time there was strict discipline in the Menzies household. Many of their exploits remained hidden, but some, to their distress, were discovered. Misdemeanours were punished by the strap; the boys claimed that they had to sit on a tin trunk afterwards to cool off. I'm not sure how little Isabel was punished, but I have no doubt that she was one of the naughtiest.

My grandmother saved up for a long time to buy a sewing machine. She was very excited when it arrived via train, horse and buggy. The children were fascinated and wondered how it worked. They looked. They wondered. It was a mystery that had to be investigated. They took it to pieces to find out . . . Whoops! All the king's horses and all the king's men couldn't put that thing back together again. So they dropped it piece by piece down a drain in the middle of the road. The punishment for that doesn't bear thinking about. (My father always claimed he was not involved – it was before his time.)

Although a Presbyterian, Grandpa became a pillar of the Methodist church in Jeparit because there was no Presbyterian church there. One Sunday, he was walking back from church with his friend Hugh Victor Mackay. 'HVM' had invented a new harvester which had been painted and decorated by my grandfather. Grandpa commented on the sermon they had just heard, which had been about 'sunshine'. He had a bright idea: 'Why not call your new harvester Sunshine?' And so it came to pass. The Sunshine Harvester factory was set up in the part of Melbourne that later became known as Sunshine.

The store and house in Jeparit where the Menzies family lived is now gone, but the town has recognised the family handsomely. There is a plaque paying tribute to my grandfather, and a town square and Thistle spire for my father.

Those years in Jeparit were a solid foundation for a markedly united and supportive family. That closeness never wavered. Without it, my father's life would have been much more difficult.

From Jeparit, the children went to school in Ballarat. Belle and Bob were there together, living with their Scottish grandmother – a mean old woman, according to them. (I only hope my grandchildren don't think that about me.)

Bob was considered clever and was made to study for long hours. In *Robert Menzies: A Life*, A.W. Martin wrote: 'The only books permanently permissible in the house were the Bible, the Presbyterian hymn book, *Ingoldsby Legends* and *Pilgrim's Progress*. But Grandma did allow bonafide school books and stood firmly over her charges: her regular order at 6.30, after an early evening meal, was "Now Robert, get to your book" (she apparently always referred to your book in the singular, as if it were some kind of universal compendium).'

Bob loved reading, so with his studies done, he went to bed and read books, illicitly smuggled in, by candlelight. The first time he heard the ominous tread of Grandma coming down the passage . . . HELP! . . . he blew out his candle. She smelt it – trouble! But he was not a slow learner, and he developed a technique of licking his fingers and grabbing the wick and holding on so the candle went out and there was no smell. To the delight of his descendants, he never lost that skill.

One night he was studying – 'slave-driven' he called it – and Belle was her usual comforting presence. She decided to make toffee on an enamel plate over the fire. They ate all they could and hid the remains under the bed. 'Nobody ever cleans under the bed,' said she confidently.

Wrong. The next day the children came home from school for lunch as usual. On the table in front of them was the plate of fluff-covered toffee: lunch.

In 1909, when their father was elected to the Victorian government, the family left Jeparit and moved to Melbourne. The following year, thanks to a scholarship, Bob began at the well-known and highly regarded school Wesley College.

The family remained close-knit – and that included the extended family. My father's cousin Douglas lived with them in Melbourne for some time. The family custom of reading aloud naturally included him. The poor boy had a stammer but Grandpa made no allowances for that. 'Don't stammer, boy.' As my father said later, this went against all the rules of psychology and everything else. 'But all I know is that it worked.' Indeed, Douglas went on to become a most distinguished and stammer-less High Court judge.

Les, the eldest son, went to the 1914–18 war, and in due course became a trade commissioner. For that reason he lived mostly in Canberra or overseas. His son, Stuart, sometimes stayed with us, and remained a good friend, although I didn't know my Uncle Les nearly as well as my other uncles and aunts. But I remember well my father's sorrow when Les died in 1953.

The second son, Frank, joined the Victorian Public Service in 1909. He enjoyed the short walk from the family home in East Melbourne through Treasury Gardens to the office in the Treasury Building. It was a longer walk to the University of Melbourne, where he studied law at night. His life became marginally easier when he bought a bicycle. By the time he joined the AIF in 1915, he had completed three years of his course. When he returned from a horrendous time at the war, he completed it. He rose to become Victorian Solicitor-General, a position he held for nearly thirty years.

Frank never lost an older brother's sense of authority. In later years, Frank once said to me, 'I feel I'm in a position to tell Bob what he needs to know,' while my father said, 'I do wish Frank wouldn't lecture me.'

In fact, my father was much in Frank's debt. After my father's death in 1978, I found a letter written by Frank in 1941 after my father had resigned as prime minister. In it, he gave Bob valuable advice about what he thought should be done or corrected, what Bob should change, perhaps, in his dealings with people. The fact that Bob kept the letter is proof of how much he valued it. As he did Frank's reprimand when he was a young boy: 'You've got a very bad temper, Bob, and you must learn to control it.' He certainly did. He became an extraordinarily patient man.

In more practical matters, Frank showed his saint-like quality. With his strict Presbyterian background, my father was scrupulous in the handling of money. So when he went into parliament he accepted with alacrity Frank's offer to take over his financial affairs. He didn't want to know what his investments were, he wanted no accusations of conflict of interest, and anyway he had no time to spare, especially when he was prime minister. And this was well before the days when members of parliament were obliged to declare their financial interests.

Although he was older, Frank lived longer than Bob, and so was able, always, to provide the friendship, support and love that Bob so much appreciated. My father dedicated his book *Afternoon Light* to 'Frank Gladstone Menzies, C.B.E. Brother, Counsellor, Friend'.

Belle and Bob were close in age and temperament. They shared the same sense of humour and drama, and they knew how to make the most out of telling a story. They were never dull.

During the 1914–18 war, Belle fell in love with a soldier, George Green. One night he told her he had two days' leave before he had to go overseas, and he had a special licence for them to be married the next day. Her father was furious, and in melodramatic style said, 'If you marry George, never darken my doorstep again.' Nothing could have been better calculated to drive her to elope with George. I well remember an enthralled audience of our daughters when she described it. It sounded just like a novel. She climbed out the window and down the ladder and went off, with only the small bag that she could carry. When she contacted her mother to ask if she would send her belongings, the answer was: 'No'.

Belle described her wedding thus:

> Apart from the Padre, two soldier witnesses were the only people present. Our only wedding gift, a Bible. After the ceremony we went to a River Tea House, where two rooms were made available for our use. Our wedding breakfast consisted of left overs from a Sunday School picnic: bacon and eggs, cream puffs and Swiss roll.

So there was Belle, cut off from her family. The only one who kept in touch with her at that time was Bob.

Belle and her parents were reconciled by the time George came back from the war, three years later. The brave – or foolhardy – pair went to Mildura, and later to Red Cliffs in northern Victoria. There George worked in the irrigation and dried-fruit industries.

Their accommodation was barely basic in that 'Land of Golden Opportunity'. One wall of their 'wooden tent' was hessian, and when it rained hard Belle would spread newspapers over the bed and furniture and put up an umbrella.

For quite a while, she was the only woman in a district of 600 men. It was far from an easy life, particularly as she had three children within twenty-seven months, but Belle still managed to help organise the creation of Baby Health Centres in Victoria.

After ten years of the pioneering life, they returned to Melbourne. Belle went to see Sidney Myer of the Myer Emporium and said, 'I've been looking at your store and notice that you have no Post Office. You should have one, and I will run it for you.' She did. George got a job as secretary of the Trustees of the Exhibition Building, and a house to go with it.

When George died in 1938 Belle applied for and got his job. Although she did it effectively and enthusiastically, she was paid considerably less because she was a woman. It did at least mean that she and her children could stay in the house.

Occasionally when my mother was away Belle, having retired, came to Canberra to keep Bob company and act as his hostess. There she was, of course, both efficient and popular. When I reflect on the fact that her earlier life was lived in such primitive conditions, I am full of admiration for the way she always dressed beautifully and looked magnificent.

Years later, on her ninetieth birthday, Belle rose arthritically to her feet and made a speech which included this piece of advice: 'You must have young friends. Your own generation just die and leave you. You *must* have young friends.'

Belle died after my father, but on his birthday. I'll bet she organised that. Peter and I and our daughters loved her, and we are enormously happy that we have two granddaughters named after her.

Syd was born ten years after Bob. His much older siblings were horrified when the little boy gave cheek to their irascible father. Worse: he got away with it! As an adult, Syd was very entertaining and a shining light for us all. He and his wife, Joyce, came to live in our house with their own small daughter, to look after my brothers and me when my parents went to England in the mid-1930s – a trip that took a long time in those days of travelling by sea.

Later they lived quite close to us, and my father 'dropped in' there often, particularly if life was difficult. At those times, I think Syd saw it as his 'duty' to cheer Bob up, which he unfailingly did.

On one occasion, when Syd and Joyce were staying at The Lodge, my father rang from his office to say he would be late, and would Syd mix the drinks. When he got home, he was handed a Syd martini. All eyes were on him.

'Well, Bob, how's the drink?' Syd asked.

'Hmm . . . Very good, Syd, but not as good as mine.'

'So what's the secret?'

'Accurate measurement, accurate measurement.'

The next night, my father rushed in late and went straight to the pantry to mix the martinis. Syd was hiding behind the door. He watched Bob carefully measure the gin and vermouth into the 'jug', then stir it and have a sip . . . Bob carefully measured more gin, stirred and tasted. Then he picked up the bottle and poured indiscriminately into the jug, added ice, stirred again and took it in to his thirsty customers. Accurate measurement indeed!

It was a great sadness for all of us when Syd died in 1971 at the age of 66. One of his daughters said to me recently, 'Family is precious.' No one appreciated that sentiment more than my father.

I think my father would have been very pleased had he lived long enough to know about the re-establishment of our family's connection with Cornwall. Some years ago, I received a letter from an Australian woman living there. Her name was Jacynth Woolven and she was secretary of the Penzance branch of the Britain-Australia Society. She asked whether it was true that my father's forebears came from Cornwall. I said that it was, and she told me that her branch wanted to put up a plaque recognising that. In due course, Peter and I went to Penzance, and I unveiled a plaque. It is on the wall of the post office. It reads:

John and Catherine Sampson lived near this site in 1840, their son John Sampson and his wife Mary Jane emigrated to Australia in 1854. Great-grandson and grandson Robert Menzies was Prime Minister of Australia from 1938–41 and 1949–1966.

The Weight and Quality of Words

Bob didn't speak at all for several years as a child. I imagine that, as the fourth child in the family, he was able to get what he wanted without having to. In Jeparit, when he went to the lolly shop clutching his penny, he would stand silently in front of the counter looking longingly at the sweet of his choice. The shopkeeper, well aware of that choice, would tease Bob and point to every other sweet on display. But Bob was strong minded, even then, and simply shook his head until the final Bull's Eye gained a vigorous nod and smile.

At the age of three, Bob relented and started to speak fluently, never to look back. (He later claimed he hadn't wanted to make a fool of himself by making mistakes.) He went to the local state school, where the teacher was Mr Livingston, known to the children as 'Daddy Livingston'. There were about thirty pupils. Flies were (and, no doubt, still are) an irritating feature of life there. But 'Daddy' remained composed, and as soon as a fly landed on his bald head he would grab it between his thumb and forefinger, squash it and drop it on the floor, all without missing a beat. At the end of the lesson there would be a collection of dead flies all around him. (It has crossed my mind that squashing flies and going on with the lesson is not entirely different from squashing interjectors and going on with a speech without missing a beat.)

The school had regular visits from the Inspector, who was treated with great respect, indeed awe. One year, 'Daddy' decided that Bob should be the one to make a little speech of thanks. When the time came, 'Daddy' announced, 'Now Robert will say a few words.'

Bob duly stepped forward and looked with terror at the large, imposing figure before him. He opened his mouth, swallowed, looked up again, closed his eyes, opened them . . . until 'Daddy' finally rescued him by saying, 'Thank you, Robert.' And that was his first speech.

One event of note was a visit to the school by a phrenologist. There is some difference of opinion about this, but when he felt Bob's head he said either 'This boy will be a barrister one day' or 'This boy will be prime minister'. Whatever the case, he was right – but did it influence the boy to do what he did?

As I have already mentioned, Grandma Menzies in Ballarat was a strict disciplinarian. One of her punishments for misdemeanours was to learn long passages from the Bible. I assume Bob was quite a naughty boy because he acquired an extensive knowledge of the Bible.

One year while he was in Ballarat, a family friend gave him a ticket to the South Street Competitions, which is an annual event for the performing arts. For the rest of his life he had a vivid recollection of sitting there on a hot day in the middle of a row of what were, to him, very large women. There was no escape. Amongst other things, he listened to twenty-seven versions of Shakespeare's 'friends, Romans, countrymen' speech from *Julius Caesar*. He learnt a lot that day. He learnt how *not* to recite and how *not* to speak in public. I wonder if he made a conscious decision then to find the best way to convey a message to an audience?

That he did learn is beyond question. Seventy years later, Father McEntee, an Australian Redemptorist priest whom I got to know in the Philippines, told me this: 'In the seminary we were trained on your father's speeches. They would put on a record of him speaking and we would analyse it. For instance, he would raise his voice, pause – almost too long – then come in with the punch line an octave lower.' Oh, yes. I can recognise that.

To his granddaughter Edwina, he wrote:

> It may amuse you to know that when I had a big speech to make in the House, I would begin by making brief notes merely as a reminder to me as to what my line of argument was to be and relying upon the moment to produce the words in which I would clothe the ideas. The night before the speech I read poetry because great poetry gives one a sense of the weight and quality of words which perhaps no other reading can do.

My father's first press secretary, Stewart Cockburn, has said: 'Few politicians, however illiterate, employed speechwriters in the 1950s, and Menzies, most literate of them all, did not need one. He disliked writing speeches before delivering them.'

While at Wesley College in Melbourne, Bob developed his love of literature and poetry. He won the Shakespeare Society prizes, involving learning by heart many hundreds of lines of the prescribed play. In other words, he had stored in that receptive brain a huge amount of the Bible, literature and poetry. The words of songs had lodged there too. It is little wonder that, after visiting and interviewing my father in England in 1967, the journalist Reginald Pound wrote: 'He can season the talk with a ready sprinkling of literary allusion and quotation.'

And so it was, always, in private conversation, in letters and in speeches. Why should a speech welcoming the Queen in 1963 deviate from this habit of a lifetime?

My Uncle Frank had a good tenor voice, and we all enjoyed listening to him sing at the piano. One of his songs was 'Passing By'. I remember it well. The poem first appeared in 1607. The music, written some three centuries later, was by Edward Purcell. The phrase from that must have been in my father's mind when he spoke to the Queen at a big gathering at Parliament House:

> . . . every man, woman and child who even sees you with a passing glimpse as you go by will remember – remember it with joy – remember it in the words of the old seventeenth-century poet who wrote, 'I did but see her passing by, and yet I love her till I die'.

How many times has this been shown on TV and commented on in newspapers and on radio for years after the event? I have never understood why he is often ridiculed for this. It seems to me to have been entirely appropriate for the occasion. People *were* waiting in the streets to see the Queen passing by, and thousands of them *did* love her. Speaking immediately after my father, Arthur Calwell, the Leader of the Opposition, agreed:

> Our speeches here are, of course, quite unnecessary to assure Her Majesty of the warmth of that welcome. It will come much more directly, much more eloquently from the millions of men, women and children who will see and be seen by her in the course of this visit.

My father's biographer, Allan Martin, put it well:

> It must be the best example in Australian studies of what E. P. Thompson once satirically called the immense condescension of the present to the past. It is in my view quite ludicrous for the memory of someone as important as Menzies to be registered primarily, for many people, with such a trivial incident.

If my father had lived to see the ABC replaying those words of his again and again and again, perhaps he would have had some sympathy for the Russian composer Rachmaninov, whose friends kept asking him to play his *Prelude in C Sharp Minor*. He got so sick of it that he wished he'd never written it.

My father made hundreds of speeches, of great variety: in parliament, electioneering, opening buildings, laying foundation stones, serious lectures given in the name of distinguished people, lectures at the University of Virginia in the United States after he had retired, after-dinner speeches. But the one that is perhaps most notable is his tribute to Churchill, which he delivered from the crypt of St Paul's Cathedral in London as Churchill's funeral cortege moved away; the hooves of horses could be heard in the background.

The words, that magnificent voice, are unforgettable. The publisher of his books, Cassell, was so impressed that it printed the speech in a limited edition, at its own request and expense. It gave most of the copies to my father to give to his family and friends; of course, he gave the first to Lady Churchill.

That speech was of enormous importance to him. He worried about it, and anguished so much that when it was over he asked his friend, Charles Lloyd Jones (junior), who happened to be in London at the time, to come and see him. 'Charles, I know you'll tell me the truth,' he said. 'Was I any good?'

Charles' reply was: 'I have never heard you make a better speech. I was proud to be Australian.'

It is extraordinary, and for me a matter of great pride, that the small boy who was so tongue-tied in Jeparit was chosen to speak to the world from St Paul's Cathedral in London on such a momentous and historic occasion.

The Greatest Show on Earth

Even by the end of my father's political career, television was not a major consideration in election campaigns. He would spend four or more weeks travelling from Cairns to Perth to Hobart to Alice Springs, and all over the place. The planes used were DC-3s, so every journey was slow and tiring. He met countless numbers of people and made up to three speeches a day, and he greatly appreciated the teas and lunches that were often provided by organisations such as the Country Women's Association.

My mother played a big part in all this. She sat on platforms and somehow stayed awake. She was so good with people that she inspired the following comment, overheard in a crowd: 'Not sure about old Pig Iron, but the little woman, she's a beaut, so he can't be too bad after all.'

My father learnt a lot from his uncle Syd Sampson. Uncle Syd went to hear Bob's first major political speech, and criticised it trenchantly afterwards. He thought it was excellent for the High Court but not for a political meeting. As he told Bob: 'A politician must take care to speak simply, introduce a little humour and, above all, keep repeating, albeit with variations in his choice of words, a few uncomplicated ideas.'

Knowing the message he wanted to get across at his meetings, my father would rarely make more than three main points in a speech. But in fact most press reports seemed to me to consist of gleeful descriptions of interjections and his replies.

Indeed, his political meetings were, like Wirth's Circus, the Greatest Show on Earth. In his book *The Measure of the Years*, he wrote of his meetings: '. . . being both crowded and ferocious and, for a man of my nature, most enjoyable'.

In September 1943 he wrote to my brother Ken:

> The election was a long-drawn-out affair consisting of at least five weeks of continuous campaigning in the course of which I spoke in five States and travelled something over seven thousand miles – 5,500 of them by air. Fadden

> also covered a lot of ground. He complained regularly that his meetings were noisy and were subjected to organised obstruction, but my own impression is that he created most of the noise by a failure to realise that interjections, properly considered, are a help and not a hindrance. Of my own fifty meetings, only two were really badly obstructed – the one in East Sydney, where the mob looked exactly like a French Revolution mob, and where, in the dark street afterwards, I had some nasty feelings before I reached safety; and the other in Fremantle, where the wharf labourers had organised a series of strong positions in the Town Hall and 'counted me out' continuously for seventy minutes! Apart from these two experiences, meetings were well attended and most friendly in character.

At a dinner not long ago, I spoke about my mother. I related her version of the end of that meeting in East Sydney:

> My husband was eased out of the mayhem by the police and I was left behind in the crowd.
>
> I managed to get close to a big strong policeman, grabbed his arm, and said: '*He* can't leave till *I* leave' . . . 'Oh alright, love.' With which my burly saviour picked me up under one arm and carried me to safety.

After that dinner, one of the guests, the recipient of a bravery award, came up to me and said, 'I know that policeman – he told me that same story.'

Rear Admiral Andrew Robertson, AO, DSC, wrote to me about another of my father's 'shows':

> . . . we attended one of his election meetings at Hornsby soon after he returned to power. That occasion makes one think of the huge changes which have come over Australia, and political life in particular. Your father and mother arrived by car – *no police* – but plenty of hecklers present – a packed hall. All, including the hecklers, stood back politely to let the P.M. through and paid him due respect. He handled them with humour and addressed their problems. One or two were politely asked to leave the hall, by the organisers, but these were no real problem and much laughter. Indeed it was a splendid evening and all seemed to enjoy themselves! Today?

However edgy we felt at the beginning of a meeting, our family – including my father – would relax with the first interjection, which usually included the tag 'Pig Iron Bob'. That had originated when waterside workers refused to load scrap iron for Japan, because of Japan's attack on China. My father, then the attorney-general, went and faced the strikers to explain that the government was not prepared to have its policy towards Japan dictated to it by the unions. The nickname stuck to him for the rest of his life. Coined as an expression of abuse, with the passage of time it became almost one of respect and affection. 'Pig Iron Bob' was a man who would stand up for what he believed was right.

In a letter to *The Sydney Morning Herald* in 1993, Larry Noye wrote:

> The Rev. Bill Hobbin told me he initiated the nickname as an agitating young Methodist minister in Wollongong in 1937.
>
> In fairness to the much misunderstood Bob Menzies, I think it should be known that Bill Hobbin's opinion of him changed. He told me that after meeting the by-then Prime Minister some years later he found him 'quite a human being'.
>
> He surely must have been. For, while knowing that Bill Hobbin had a part in the vociferous chant that the PM copped at rowdy electioneering meetings, he engaged him to lead Freedom from Hunger work under government auspices.

Less alarming was a meeting I remember in Brisbane, at which a man, gesturing aggressively and yelling loudly, climbed onto the platform while my father was speaking. Senator Neil O'Sullivan swiftly rose from his seat, stepped across and threw him off. Cheers all round.

Wild meetings were the exception. Most meetings were reasonably good-humoured, and my father's witty answers always got a laugh from everyone – except, maybe, the interjector.

'I wouldn't vote for you if you were the Archangel Gabriel,' someone once yelled out at a meeting.

'If I were the Archangel Gabriel,' my father replied, 'you would not be in my electorate.'

He did have a real problem with women hecklers, because their voices were often hard to hear and understand. He developed what would now be regarded as a somewhat sexist technique to get over the problem. Instead of answering the (not understood) question, he would simply refer to 'the lady in the red hat – I recognise it as the same one that you were wearing at my last meeting here'. Or he'd say, 'My goodness, my friend down here is in good voice tonight – and is that a new hairstyle?' Sooner or later, the woman would get sick of it and shut up.

Recently, I met a man who told me his father used to take him to those meetings when he was a boy. They would get there at six o'clock – the starting time was eight o'clock – and sit in the front row with their sandwiches. One night, a woman kept yelling and waving her hand in the air. Eventually, my father stopped, looked at her and said, 'Of course, madam, it's down the passage on the right.' The young boy must have loved that one.

Another woman who kept interjecting was silenced with this: 'Madam, I have no objection to your speaking in this hall, provided you do so some other night or that you pay half the cost of the hiring of it tonight.'

The calmest meetings in the country were in the seat of Denison, Tasmania. The local member was Athol Townley, a pharmacist who, during the Depression years, had always been generous to people who couldn't afford to pay him. The result was that any political meeting for the Liberal Party in his electorate had a considerable presence of 'bodyguards' – ardent supporters from the waterside worker community. Any interjector would quickly feel a heavy hand on the shoulder.

It was in Tasmania, at the end of a particularly gruelling campaign, that the audience seemed to sway up and down in front of my father's eyes. 'It was sheer technique that kept me going,' he said. With his 'technique' I've no doubt he got away with it.

Election day was spent going round his electorate of Kooyong, where he'd visit every polling booth. During one election he reached the booth in Pakington Street, Kew, in the late afternoon. There was a '*Herald* boy' selling the evening paper further down the road. He had red hair, and in those days redheads were nearly always called 'Blue'. So my father called out to him: 'Hey, Blue, bring me a *Herald*.' The boy came up and the paper was duly handed over and paid for.

As the boy turned to go, another man put a hand on his shoulder and stopped him. 'Do you know the man you just sold that paper to?' he asked.

The boy gave a bemused shake of the head.

'He is the Prime Minister of Australia.'

With his mouth open in surprise, the boy looked back at the big, impressive PM, turned and ran down the hill, yelling, 'Hey, Mum! He's the Prime Minister and he knows my name!'

My grandfather James Menzies spent every election day at the polling booth at Trinity Grammar School in Kew. My father described such a day in a letter to Ken in 1943:

> He got to the booth at 8 a.m. as usual and was on 'how to vote' card duty all day. Syd went across during the day, but was very soon ordered off as a nincompoop! The old man was performing his usual stunt of taking Labor tickets out of the hands of people and tearing them up and dropping them over the fence, and using honeyed words as he pressed my own ticket into more or less reluctant

> hands! Unfortunately, one result of the day's exertions is that Father is now in bed with a heavy cold, but even in a recumbent position he can still reconstruct the political world to his own complete satisfaction. There is no doubt that he is a marvel.

During one election campaign, I travelled around Australia with my father. A prized souvenir is a verse handed to me by a journalist on a plane in Queensland:

The bonnie belles of Bundaberg
Chew sugar from the stalk
If Heather Menzies copied them
She'd have less time to talk.

Of course, I was brainwashed. I sat through dozens of meetings and heard only one side. I knew all the arguments. At the end of one election day I can remember saying, 'Well, really, Dad, I can't see how anyone could vote for anyone else.'

As he pointed out, just over fifty per cent would do him fine.

Over the years, of course, he did considerably better than that. He won seven federal elections in a row.

Becoming Prime Minister

Eileen Lenihan – known as 'Lennie' – worked in Parliament House for years, including in the office of the Prime Minister Mr Lyons. She became my father's private secretary, and was succeeded in that post by Hazel Craig. The two women were close friends. The account which follows of the circumstances in which my father became prime minister has come to me from Hazel, who heard the whole story from Lennie, and wrote it down for me:

> In 1934 Sir John Latham resigned from parliament and left the Prime Minister Mr Lyons without an Attorney-General. Menzies was the Attorney-General of Victoria and

had, at times, been Acting Premier. Lyons invited him to contest the seat of Kooyong, left vacant by Latham, with the promise that he would become the federal Attorney-General upon election. Menzies won the seat and was so appointed. At a meeting of the United Australia Party he was also elected Deputy Leader of the party.

In the late 1930s the government decided to bring in a national insurance scheme, and a committee of senior ministers was set up to handle the issue. It included Lyons, Menzies and Page. Menzies believed that the scheme would benefit the Australian people and went to the trouble to explain it to his electorate, assuring the voters that it was coming into being; Menzies was responsible for drafting the bill for Parliament.

In 1939 the committee had a final meeting in Hobart. At the weekend its members flew from Hobart to Canberra via Melbourne, where Menzies left the group to spend the weekend with his family. That evening in Canberra, Mr Lyons invited the other members of the committee to dinner, during which they discussed the scheme and decided to scrap it. Without talking to Menzies to explain their decision, the PM went on the radio and announced it.

The following Monday, Menzies went back to Canberra. Lennie was going through correspondence with the PM when the phone rang. It was Menzies, asking if he could come around and see him. Lyons put his head in his hands and said, 'If Menzies resigns, I don't know what I'm going to do.'

Of course, Menzies did resign as Attorney-General and Deputy Prime Minister. What else could he do? He felt terrible about letting down his Kooyong constituents. Moreover, he had been treated with great discourtesy by his colleagues, and could not ignore it.

When Lyons died soon after this the UAP had no deputy leader, and so the Leader of the Country Party, Dr Earle Page, became Prime Minister. The party met as soon as possible and chose Menzies as their leader. Page therefore was PM for only nineteen days. He resented being deposed. He had disliked Menzies for years so I suppose that must have been the finishing touch.

(If I can write as lucidly as this when I am 97 it will be a miracle.)

Some members of the Lyons family have blamed my father for causing or hastening Lyons' death. I wish they had been aware of Lennie's account of what actually happened over the whole national insurance issue. I only heard it myself recently.

Even more recently, my attention has been drawn to the account of Lyons' last few weeks given by the former Clerk of the House, Frank Green, in his book *Servant of the*

House. Green writes that Lyons was under great pressure over the insurance scheme from the Temple Court group of Melbourne businessmen, 'which controlled the United Australia Party'. Lyons was 'instructed' not to proclaim the Insurance Act without the group's permission.

Green, who was an old and trusted friend of Lyons from their student days in Hobart, says he provided a haven for Lyons on two occasions at this time. Of the first one, Green writes: 'When he came to me from the Cabinet room I could see he was under great nervous tension, and almost hysterical.' On the second occasion, according to Green, Lyons said he wanted to resign and end the torture.

At Easter 1939, Lyons sent for Green and told him he was going to Sydney to rest. In his book Green observes that Lyons 'had reached such a state of nervous strain that he couldn't have rested anywhere'. Then, Green writes, 'a few minutes later he was on his way to Sydney by car but along the road he had a heart attack and died in a Sydney hospital a day later'.

These two accounts, by Lennie and Frank Green, have done much to dispel the concern I've always felt over my father being blamed for putting unreasonable pressure on Lyons. I am convinced that my father always supported his leader in every way he could. My mother certainly believed that too, quite emphatically.

Parliament

After some years as a barrister my father went into parliament. He took with him some of the customs of the bar, and one of those – calling people by their surnames – proved to be a big mistake. Even legal colleagues who were good friends had always been 'Dixon', 'Fullagar' and so on. It's possible that this habit contributed to his departure from the prime ministership in 1941.

It is important for people who hold any high office to have at least one person who will tell them unpalatable truths. The most valuable person for my father in this regard was his brother Frank. There is no question that Bob took note of his advice – particularly about the use of surnames – and, at least by the time I was old enough to notice, he seemed to me to be on good terms with his fellow parliamentarians of all persuasions. In any case, he respected them. He firmly believed that most people went into parliament for the right reasons: to represent their constituents, and to strive for the things they believed in.

During his first term as PM, he particularly valued the friendship, loyalty and support of Jim Fairbairn, Henry Gullett and Geoffrey Street – his three ministers who were killed in an air crash in 1940. I quote from *Afternoon Light*:

> This was a dreadful calamity, for my three colleagues were my close and loyal friends; each of them had a place not only in my Cabinet, but in my heart. I shall never forget that terrible hour; how I felt that, for me, the end of the world had come.

Earle Page was a different story altogether. (Is it irrelevant to note that he was born early on Christmas Day in Grafton, which explains his name, Earle Christmas Grafton Page? Yes, of course it is, but I can't resist it.) In April 1939, Dr Page made an attack on my father. The violence of that attack can be measured by its description in *The Sydney Morning Herald*, itself no friend of my father: it was 'a violation of the decencies of debate without parallel in the annals of the Federal Parliament'. (It was child's play compared with parliament as we know it in 2013.)

Dr Page had listed three episodes which, he said, gave him no basis of confidence that my father possessed maximum courage, loyalty or judgement. The most obnoxious of Dr Page's charges was the last: that, in the middle of the Gallipoli campaign, and having been in the military for some years, my father resigned his commission and did not go overseas. 'If he cannot satisfactorily and publicly explain to a very great body of people in Australia, who did participate in the war, his failure to do so,' said Dr Page, 'he will not be able to get that maximum effort out of the people in the event of war.'

In fact, my father had served the necessary stint of compulsory military training in the Melbourne University Rifles, and attained the rank of lieutenant. He held his commission until his mandatory period of service was over. He did not resign.

My mother was in the House of Representatives when Page made his attack on my father. When she realised what he was saying, she stood and stared at him for a full minute – with all eyes on her – and slowly walked out of the House. After that, she ignored him whenever she found herself in his presence.

I quote from a letter written by Page's daughter-in-law to my brother Ken in 1979:

> I happened to be Sir Earle Page's secretary in April 1939 and typed the fateful speech for the eighth or ninth time, taking the paragraph in and out many times. Everybody involved at the centre like Lady Page, Tom Patterson, myself advised against this, knowing that it would reflect more on himself for using it than on your father. But Archie Cameron [MHR for Barker 1935–56, Speaker from 1950], who was a very militaristic Highland non-gentleman with very authoritative urges, kept on at him until he persuaded him. I happened to be standing behind your mother in the Chamber that day and saw her colour change, so I know what she went through on that occasion. Of course there was nothing anyone close to him could do – he was such a strong willed man but he regretted it for the rest of his life . . . He often used to say to me wistfully, 'You know Dame Pattie just never speaks to me anywhere!' I always replied, 'Well why would she?'

Unlike my mother, my father put that all behind him. Page became a minister in his Cabinet and they worked effectively together.

•

Eric Harrison was a good friend and loyal colleague always. In 1941 there was great dissension between the coalition partners. The press disliked Menzies, and everything was gloomy for him. He decided he should resign. Wal Fife describes in his book *A Country Liberal* what occurred:

> Eric Harrison's wife Mary, who had been ill for some time, died in Sydney early in the morning of 26th August. In the light of the crisis in the Government, Harrison was anxious to get back to Canberra. His wife was buried the day after her death, 27th August. Shirley, the second of his three daughters (she was fifteen years of age at the time), recalled her father saying goodbye to her and her sisters, Joan and Helen, immediately after the funeral, stepping into the black Commonwealth Buick, and returning to Canberra. Harrison, whom Allan Martin calls Menzies' 'staunchest supporter', was hopeful of persuading Menzies to stay, but he arrived in Canberra too late.

My father was reluctant to let Eric Harrison go to London as High Commissioner in 1956 because he valued him so much at home; but loyalty goes both ways, and that was Harrison's heartfelt wish. So he went, and did a good job there for Australia.

Our families knew each other well, and the Harrisons were particularly hospitable to my brother Ken when he was in the army and stationed in Sydney for a while during the war. For that reason, my father wrote to Ken (who by that time was in Bougainville) with a full description of the wedding of Eric Harrison's daughter, Joan. My father was Leader of the Opposition at the time. The letter included the following:

> I was assigned an official part in the proceedings by taking the new Mrs Harrison in. I don't think you have ever met her, but she looked extraordinarily handsome in dark blue velvet, with myself in a boiled shirt [his usual description of the dreaded white tie and tails] providing the necessary background.
>
> The wedding took place at St Stephen's Church in Macquarie Street and the wedding breakfast at the Pickwick Club in Castlereagh Street.
>
> The officiating Minister was the Reverend George Cowie, who at his prime was the Moderator of the Presbyterian Church in NSW and who is now stationed at Surry Hills, up among Eddie Ward's constituents. He is a very old friend of Eric Harrison and of Sir Frederick Stewart, much given to violent political views, not entirely hostile to a well-poured whisky and soda, unexpected in what he has to say, and with some of the oddities that old men of his type occasionally permit themselves. He is a smallish man, with glasses and an Aberdonian accent.

The wedding service was absolutely unique in my experience. Some of its more salient features I have now reduced to verse, of which I enclose a copy. The staggering thing is that the verse is almost literally correct. The old boy's notion was that he should sandwich in between the formal portions of the wedding ceremony a series of homilies to the happy couple, all delivered with the greatest informality and, to some extent at least, for the benefit of the substantial number of people present in the Church. Let me give you a few examples:

He took great joy in pronouncing the bridegroom's name, which in the true manner he did as if it were 'Doonald Stairling Taylor'. If he pronounced the name once I am sure he did so a dozen times, varying it by addressing him as 'young man'. About the third time he pronounced the name he suddenly paused and said, 'Aye, "Stairling", that's a good name. It was at Stirling that we Scots won the Battle of Bannockburn.'

In advising the bride and bridegroom that there were things in life which were of prime importance and which only God could make, he instanced the fresh air and sunlight, interrupting himself, however, sufficiently to deliver a eulogy on the beneficial effects of the sun's rays upon the human body and to make a side remark to the effect that he was a believer in fresh air and that in his opinion a great deal of the ill health of Sydney was due to air conditioning. You can imagine it was difficult to keep a straight face.

Later on he looked at the bridegroom and said, 'Well, Doonald Stairling Taylor, you are in the Navy. Let us all hope that in a year the fighting may be over and that we may have peace and (with a glance in my direction) new rulers in Australia.'

He then went on to say something about the symbolism of the wedding breakfast, the first meal in married life. This gave him a chance to urge upon the bridegroom and bride the cultivation of friendly and companionable qualities. I almost rocked from my seat when he proceeded to say: 'After all, ye know, Jesus Christ himself was a companionable man; he liked his cup of tea.'

At long last the Service ended and after this fascinating mixture of religion, ceremonial, politics, bad history, and general observations, we adjourned to the breakfast. There, in introducing first myself and Sir Frederick Stewart, he proposed the toast to the Bride and Bridegroom, the old man elaborated his beliefs. He got one in on Fred Stewart (who is a prominent Methodist) by explaining that Scotland had remained free of the curse of Methodism because all the Methodists were killed at Bannockburn.

He made no secret of his political views and demanded to know why he should not take the chair for me at meetings in Sydney. He even ran the risk of a prosecution for heresy in the Councils of the Church by telling some of us that in his opinion the miracle of turning the water into wine might be attributed to the fact that wedding festivals in Palestine lasted for seven days and that by the sixth day the guests had taken so much wine that the host could easily substitute water without being detected.

I don't want you to think by all this that the wedding was a raree show. It really went off very well, with an immense amount of friendship being displayed all round.

Doonald Stairling Taylor, mon,
Ye've gi'en me sic a joy
To stand up here and marry ye,
A bright-eyed naval boy.

But hark ye now to my advice –
Be pleasant to our Joan,
Eat up your parritch every day
And never drink alone.

Pray for the war to end next year
And for the Leeberal Party,

Avoid conditioned air, and you
Will grow up hale and hearty.

The scriptures tell us, Donald lad,
That Christ drank tea with passion
Alas He could not buy it, now
That Keane's cut down the ration!

Take the wee lassie in your arrms
And set your senses whirling
Thank God we killed the Methodists
In bluidy fight at Stirling!

NOW, BACK TO BUSINESS, I DECLARE
YOU MARRIED, WITHOUT BLUNDER,
AND THOSE WHOM COWIE'S MADE A PAIR
LET NO MAN PUT ASUNDER

My father enjoyed real friendship with several other fellow MPs. He was overheard saying to Artie Fadden, 'If I could talk to that man as you did, Artie, I'd give my right arm.' Artie Fadden and Athol Townley were frequent visitors to The Lodge, and provided the necessary laughs when times were tough.

Hubert Opperman – 'Oppy' – a champion cyclist, stood for the seat of Corio as a Liberal candidate. When he won by 139 votes, my father sent him a telegram: 'First the frame, then the wheels, then the chain, then the handlebars, and, at last, the seat.' Later, when Oppy returned from his first trip overseas as a minister, he sent a telegram to my father in which he quoted from a well-known song: '"It's a great big beautiful world we live in" – but it looks best from home.'

In fact, there are very few names I can leave out. Two men who were of particular support when he retired and after he had a stroke were Alick Downer (senior) and Doug Anthony.

But friendship was not confined to his own side of politics. This exchange of letters with his opponent John Curtin shows how warm their relationship was:

To John Curtin, 29th August 1941

My dear John,

I have ceased to be Prime Minister and we shall therefore no longer be opposite numbers at the table.

I want to thank you for two years and four months in which my task, always difficult, has frequently been rendered easier and at all times more tolerable by your magnanimous and understanding attitude.

Your political opposition has been honourable and your personal friendship a pearl of great price.

Yours sincerely . . .

To Robert Menzies, 1941

Dear Bob,

Thank you for your letter. I appreciate it more than I can say. On my part I thank you wholeheartedly for the consideration and courtesy which never once failed in your dealings with me. I wish you good health and fair going. Your personal friendship is something I value, as I hope and know you do, as a very precious thing.

Yours faithfully . . .

My father was also on very good terms with Ben Chifley, and it made no difference which one of them was prime minister. For example, Chifley would knock on the door and say, 'This is a good whodunit, Bob. Thought you might enjoy it.' Or a phone call: 'I'm sick of it all, Bob. Come round and have a yarn.' Or one of them would give a signal across the despatch table and they would both walk casually behind the Speaker's chair. 'Can't you control your people?' Those things worked both ways.

As prime minister, my father always told his opposite number before he made any important announcement in the House. With his great respect for parliament, he believed that was where all announcements of national importance should be made. Yet solemnity was by no means always the order of the day, even in parliament. My father once said, 'The safety and peace of the world depend on whether the people who can laugh are in the majority.' His sense of humour was appreciated by most members – but maybe not all.

In 1956 he came to the rescue of a Labor MP who was in trouble for using the word 'bloody'. Amid laughter, Menzies proposed to the Deputy Speaker: 'Might I suggest that the matter be brought to an honourable conclusion by you directing Hansard to omit the word of emphasis and substitute "sanguinary"?'

He also loved it when the joke was turned on him. One day during question time, Allan Fraser, the Labor member for Eden Monaro, asked the following: 'My gentle St. Andrew's question is addressed to the Prime Minister. I heard that the right honourable gentleman lamented in Melbourne yesterday that Australians call him Menzies. [The Scottish pronunciation is Mingies]. Does he really think that is what they call him?'

'The answer to that question, sir, is "No"', he replied, 'I am not unacquainted with what I am called. The other night when I was arriving for a St. Andrew's night dinner in Melbourne, I was greeted in familiar and stentorian tones by a group of gentlemen on the footpath, by the soubriquet "Pig-iron". On the other hand, I am happy to report that as

I am driven around in the cities I frequently find the driver of a truck pulling up alongside me, looking over at me and saying: "Good on you, Bob."'

That master of the interjection, Jim Cope (Labor), called out: 'He ought to be pinched for drunken driving.' My father enjoyed that so much that he invited Jim round for a drink afterwards.

My mother received a letter from Jim Cope after my father died, in which he wrote:

> Prior to my entering the Federal Parliament in May 1955, I imagined Mr Menzies, as he was then, to be a supercilious arrogant person. However in a short time I discovered to the contrary that Bob, as he was more fondly known to me, possessed a warm and friendly personality plus a very keen sense of humour. I recall with pride that whenever we met by chance in the lobbies, he always spared a few minutes for a little chat.
>
> My most treasured possession and one which I shall cherish for the rest of my days is an autographed copy with a personal message to me of *Afternoon Light*, a present from Bob.
>
> The eulogistic expressions by Her Majesty the Queen and heads of world nations and numerous friends particularly in the political field leave no doubt that Sir Robert

> was a great statesman, respected and liked despite any inevitable political differences.
>
> Sir Robert's name joins the list of immortals in World and Australian politics. As you have lost a great mate in life, Australia has lost a great man.

When my brother Ken and his wife, Marjorie, had twins, Frank Forde, a former Labor MP, minister and prime minister, wrote to 'Dear Bob' and included this generous comment: 'Your grandsons, Donald and Geoffrey, have a very distinguished Grandfather; and in the years that lie ahead, I feel sure that they will be very proud to point to your record of distinguished service as Prime Minister for such a lengthy period.'

Eddie Ward was a constant critic, indeed often quite nasty. But I have been told on good authority that on one occasion, when my father spoke eloquently and movingly on a condolence motion, Eddie turned to Arthur Calwell and said, 'When I die, all I ask is that Bob should get up and say, "He was loved by all."' There was nothing wrong with Ward's sense of humour.

Well, when Eddie died Bob did get up and say some remarkably generous things, if not that he was loved by all. On the way out of the House he was stopped by Jim Killen, a Liberal MP, who asked, 'How could you speak so kindly about Eddie when he has said such appalling things about you?'

'Killen, there's something good to be said about every human being,' Bob replied. 'Who knows, in the course of time, we might even think of something good to say about you.'

Jim enjoyed and cherished that, and happily passed it on to me.

Ken Ingram, the Hansard Principal Parliamentary Reporter, wrote to me in 1978: 'Across the floor of the Parliament many hard things are said and Sir Robert could hit as hard as anyone, but usually his remarks were tinged with good humour – a quality that seems to be fast disappearing from parliamentary life.'

Yes. Thinking about parliament and parliamentarians and how things worked in my father's day in the old Parliament House, I can't help noticing the sharp contrasts with today's practice and personal behaviour. In those days, proceedings were usually marked by the good humour noted by Ken Ingram, even when someone like Eddie Ward was involved. This now seems to be lacking. Attacks of a personal and bitter nature seem to be more frequent than they were. These days, there often seems to be a nastiness at question time. There is an avoidance of answering questions, and 'Dorothy Dixers' are used as an excuse for abuse of opponents and electioneering speeches. This applies to both sides of politics.

My father would ask a Labor backbencher for a quiet drink in his office. Could this happen now? It seems to me that in those days there was some prevailing and all-embracing sense of fellowship. Of course, it helped that the old Parliament House was small, and that members mingled willy-nilly with each other in the lobbies and lavatories and dining room. They didn't have their own offices staffed by people with the same political views as themselves.

I wonder how much the configuration and size of the present Parliament House has to do with this change. Do the members all now retreat into their own offices, and so have fewer opportunities to get to know each other at a personal and social level? Whatever the reason for the change in atmosphere, I believe it can only be deplored.

The Public Service: Vital Contributors

My father had enormous admiration for the Westminster system of government. He regarded it as a privilege to be a member of parliament, and treated the House of Representatives with respect. This respect extended to the Public Service – from the heads of departments to the drivers of Commonwealth cars – and I have no doubt that it was reciprocated.

The question of the political views and affiliations of individual public servants arose immediately after the 1949 election. The head of the Prime Minister's Department, Allen Brown – who had been appointed by the previous

Labor government – told my father that one of his senior officers was the president of a branch of the local Labor Party. My father's reaction was: 'Can he be trusted to give me professional advice? I don't care what he's president of.'

Another man from his department came to see him, and it was the opposite story.

'I am so pleased you won,' the man said. 'I voted for you.'

'In that case,' said my father, 'you're no use to me.'

His first press secretary, Stewart Cockburn, has written:

> He disarmed me in my interview for the job, for which I had been invited to apply. When I volunteered that I had been a Labor voter until 1949 he replied: 'I'm not interested in how you vote, my boy. All I want to know is: Can you do the job? Can you be loyal?'

Speaking to members of his department at their 1949 Christmas party, my father said: 'What you do out of hours is your business. We are the politicians and we make the political decisions. We want from you the best professional advice you can give.' He got that professional advice. And great loyalty. After a while, word went around and no one talked to him about their political views.

Barry Jones, in his book *A Thinking Reed*, put it much better than I ever could:

> When Menzies became Prime Minister again in December 1949 he retained most of Chifley's senior advisers. When colleagues urged Menzies to remove Coombs, he replied, 'I have any number of people around me who will tell me what they think I want to hear. I need to have access to people who will tell me the opposite.' Arthur Fadden, his Treasurer, took the same view.

Prime ministers and ministers today take a very different approach. They fill their offices with many more advisers than there used to be, and almost always with acknowledged political supporters. When my father became prime minister again in 1949, there was only a handful of people in his office, and they all came from the Prime Minister's Department. Many had worked loyally for his Labor predecessors. My father – as did other ministers – always had a departmental officer as his secretary. Without exception, those men worked for him with efficiency and loyalty. Perhaps that job was a stepping stone to greater things, because most of them went on to have interesting and successful careers.

Allen Brown remained as head of the Prime Minister's Department until 1959, ten years after my father became prime minister, and was awarded a knighthood in 1956. The two men got on well. Years later, referring to my father, Sir Allen wrote: 'A clear proposition was always dealt with promptly and a decision once made never came unstuck.'

Sir Allen was succeeded by John Bunting, who was a career officer in the department. My father once described Sir John (as he later became) as 'the Prince of Public Servants'. After his retirement, Sir John wrote a book, *R.G. Menzies: A Portrait*, which gives a warm and first-hand description of his former boss and how he worked. Sir John also became chairman of the Menzies Foundation, which was set up by public subscription after my father died as a form of memorial. The Foundation continues to thrive, and the postgraduate scholarships it offers attract outstanding applicants. It has also been responsible for much valuable medical research.

There is no doubt that my father was fortunate to have two men of such high calibre as his chief advisers.

For eighteen months after his re-election in 1949 he had no press secretary; indeed, he couldn't see the need for one. However, he was eventually persuaded otherwise, and the position was filled by the journalist Stewart Cockburn, mentioned earlier. Stewart was a most congenial character but was inclined to have a serious demeanour. My father commented that he looked as if he had the weight of the world on his shoulders. Of course, he became known as 'Atlas'.

Then there was Hugh Dash, a journalist and larrikin. Years later another journalist who knew my father well commented: 'There was no one who better enjoyed the company of a larrikin than Menzies.' That, perhaps, explains why my father not only tolerated 'Hughie' but had a good rapport with him, and happily – no, resignedly – topped up from his own pocket Hughie's overseas travelling allowance so he could provide adequate 'hospitality' for the press. Hughie certainly maintained a bridge between them and his boss.

An element in the good rapport between Hughie and my father was that each knew the other enjoyed a joke against himself. Not that Hughie, though he was regarded as a sort of court jester, was given to making jokes against the boss.

My father liked teasing newsmen about their writing. Once, on an overseas trip, he and Hughie were together at a conference; the official language was French, but some Greek was also spoken. My father described it afterwards (in Hughie's presence): 'Having only some French and little Greek I felt uneasy. However, looking down the table, I was vastly comforted. There was Hughie – no French, no Greek . . . and very little English.'

Ray Maley, his next press secretary, is best described by extracts from the letter my father wrote to Ray's widow, Jean, some years after Ray's death:

Ray had a close and intimate knowledge of both politics and the Press. His advice to me was always based on a close understanding of the problems involved, and, I have no doubt, saved me from many errors during the time that he was with me.

I might perhaps illustrate his great wisdom by one simple story.

Coming back from my annual visit overseas and landing at the Sydney airport at 7 o'clock in the morning after a broken night, I always felt terribly embarrassed at having to go in to be interviewed by a lot of Press boys who, naturally, hoped that I would put a foot wrong at a time when I was really not fit to think straight, or to speak straight, after a very exhausting journey.

The time came when Ray said to me on the way back to Australia: 'I want to give you a little advice. I think that when you arrive at this early hour in Sydney, you ought to permit me to tell the Press that you will not be giving an interview but will make a very brief statement without questions. But that after you have gone to Canberra that night and had a decent night's rest, you would be very happy to give them a full Press and Television interview on the next afternoon in Canberra.'

Nobody had ever suggested this to me before, but I naturally seized upon it as a very sensible thing, provided that Ray could sell it to the Press. He did. I went into the interview room on arrival and spoke for two or three minutes and it was then announced to them that after I had had a decent night and they had been able to think up questions they wanted to put to me, I would give a full Press interview at Canberra on the following afternoon. I did this, to everybody's satisfaction.

My mind was clear and I enjoyed the interviews. They had had time to work out their questions and so, I hope, they enjoyed the interviews . . .

Ray was a man with a deep knowledge of politics and political issues, a rare understanding of the task that a Prime Minister had, and great wisdom in the advice that he gave . . . His death, as I have said, was a great blow to me and made my task thereafter more difficult and, in some ways, more frustrating.

It is a matter of no small joy to me that your sons should maintain such an intelligent interest in public affairs . . . each of them could make a great contribution to clear thinking in public places.

In all their remarkable development, they have had the advantage of guidance and encouragement from a very remarkable mother.

I hope that they will each save a copy of this letter as a reminder of what their father meant to me, and what

> I think was his great contribution to the intelligence and clearness of public life.

My father's personal private secretary was also a public servant from his department.

The first one I remember was Lennie (Eileen Lenihan). In 1936 she was working for the Treasurer, Richard Casey. Prime Minister Lyons needed a new stenographer, and Casey agreed to let Lennie move to the PM's office, saying, 'This is the most unselfish thing I have ever done.'

She was a great personality, and efficient and clever. She was probably the only person since my father's school days who had the temerity to suggest: 'Perhaps a different word might be better there, Mr Menzies; what about . . . ?'

My father's only complaint about Lennie was her tendency to kleptomania when it came to pencils. Every time she came into his office she would pick up a pencil from his desk, use it for taking dictation or making notes, then absentmindedly take it with her. One day he bought a whole new box of pencils, put it on his desk and called her in as often as possible. At the end of the day the box was empty. He called her in yet again and asked: 'Lennie, where are the twenty-four pencils I bought this morning?' As usual in his office, life was not entirely real or earnest.

Lennie and my father suited each other well. They were

both happy to work till well after midnight, but had no great love of early rising. Lennie's successor and great friend, Hazel Craig, told me a lot about her. Hazel wondered if my father could have created the Liberal Party without Lennie. They both had *enthusiasm* for the project – a vital component – as well as similar working hours.

More than once Lennie worked with my father till nearly four a.m., then walked from our house in Kew to her place in Hawthorn. She made all the arrangements for meetings with representatives of the organisations that eventually agreed to form the Liberal Party. The Liberal Party owes her a great deal.

Lennie once told me about her favourite piece of correspondence from her time with my father. There was a man who wrote often. Unfortunately, he had some mental affliction, and at one stage went into an asylum. When he came out he wrote, triumphantly: 'Well, it's all very well, Mr Menzies, but I've got a certificate to prove I'm sane, and that's more than you've got.'

In 1934 Hazel Craig came to Canberra to sit for the Commonwealth exam. She joined the Australian Public Service as a stenographer. Hazel was competent and discreet and had an equable temperament and sense of humour. Those qualities, and more, saw her moved to Parliament House. For thirty years she worked for successive prime ministers: Lyons,

Menzies, Curtin, Chifley and Menzies again. Political views didn't come into it. She was my father's secretary during the whole time of his second prime ministership, from 1949 to 1966. She remained with him for ten years after he retired. Neither of my parents could have coped without her. Luckily for me, she remembered everything.

Hazel was always part of my father's delegation on his journeys overseas. It was she who wielded 'the Boss's camera' at the Coronation of Queen Elizabeth II. Having had only ten or fifteen minutes' instruction from him, that took courage. When they went to Cairo at the time of the Suez crisis in 1956, she was the guardian of the 'medical box', in case of emergencies, put together by Dr Cedric Shaw in London.

Every time my father had a birthday or won an election, he would receive an avalanche of mail. Hazel survived all of that. But in 1963, when he was created a Knight of the Thistle, the thought of the thousands of congratulatory messages he would receive was too much for her to bear. She said firmly: 'I resign!' She was ignored. The CBE she herself was awarded in 1964 was well earned.

Also important in the scheme of things were the Commonwealth car drivers. In Canberra they were sometimes inveigled into helping at The Lodge – not always to their joy. Things like feeding the ducks and chooks, or stoking the boiler – all of which my mother would do quite happily too. Wally Dunn, Alf Stafford and then Ray Coppin were particularly good when it came to grandchildren. One summer, Peter and I and our daughters were at the beach with my brother and his family when a photographer from the *Canberra Times* walked along taking happy snaps. He took one of our youngest daughter Elizabeth (known to us as Sibby), holding hands with her cousin Geoffrey. They were naked and walking towards the water. He was three and she was two. The result was a photo in the paper – from behind – of Geoffrey and his cousin Elizabeth (for obvious reasons I didn't give their surnames). Having watched Sibby playing in the blow-up paddling pool at The Lodge, Ray said he could recognise her easily in the photo. Ray continued to be a helpful friend, even after my parents left Canberra. In Sydney, Herb South was very much part of the team. In Melbourne it was Peter Pearson.

Peter drove my father around for years, including after he retired to Melbourne. He became rather like another son. They were at ease in each other's company. Once, on his return to Melbourne after some time away, my father got into the car – front seat, as usual – then turned to Peter and said, 'By Jove, lad, you've put on a bit of condition since last time I was here!'

'Well, Sir Robert, I thought the car had been a bit unbalanced for a while, so I decided to even it up.'

From Dame Pattie in the back seat: 'You deserved that, Bob.'

When my father died, Peter sent flowers with the message: 'A wonderful friend and mate for many years.'

One story I've been told illustrates perfectly the deep respect my father had for the Public Service, and his sensitivity to where the boundaries of responsibility lay. The wife of Bob Furlonger, a senior officer in the Department of Foreign Affairs, had serious health problems, so they decided it would suit them better to be in Australia. He therefore applied for a job in the Prime Minister's Department. The job went to someone else. The next time Bob saw my father, some years later, he was greeted with this: 'I told Bunting that you were the man for that job, but I couldn't dictate to him.'

The Press

There was always a strong impression that my father hated the press, later media. Well, yes and no. As with all groups of people there are those you like and those you don't.

He certainly found it hard to warm to *The Sydney Morning Herald*. Early in his public life he became aware that the newspaper disliked him. It attacked him relentlessly for years – so much so that, in 1960, he amused himself by writing his own obituary as it might appear in that paper:

> *What They Will Say*
> We announce today, without gloating but not without satisfaction, the death of the former Prime Minister, Robert Gordon Menzies.

As a newspaper of record, we feel it to be our duty to convey this news to the public. But as an independent newspaper of rare and discriminating judgment, we feel it to be equally our duty to speak the truth concerning the deceased statesman.

Fairness, our constant watchword, requires that we should record that Mr Menzies's notorious failure stemmed from two circumstances for which he was not entirely to blame. He was not born of wealthy parents. He was not born in Sydney.

Possessed as he was of a certain rudimentary native intelligence, he clearly set out to overcome, though alas without much success, these initial disabilities. In particular, he acquired and practised a certain skill in words which led – we feel bound to concede it – to a somewhat singular lucidity of speech. This made him difficult to misreport. But we have never been deterred by difficulties; in this connection our readers will share our pride in the way in which we overcame them.

If there is one thing about the right honourable gentleman which our more docile readers will, over many years, have learned to understand, is that he spoke much, but achieved little. To him, the logical argument or statement (and we use the word 'logical' only for the purposes of our argument) was sufficient. Consequent action was unimportant.

True, it has occasionally been said by bigoted Victorians that, as Leader of the Opposition from 1943–1949, he amalgamated fourteen scattered political groups into one Liberal Party, endowed them with a coherent and constructive policy, secured an enduring partnership with the Country Party, and swept our friends of the Labour Party out of office for more than a decade.

But wise and unprejudiced men will not be unduly affected by such meretricious arguments. The truth is not to be overthrown by exceptions, particularly if they are recorded South of the Murray.

We have always specialised in opposition, and are therefore not unduly impressed by the labours of our rivals in this field.

The real test is what Mr Menzies did as Prime Minister. And this test, as we have been saying for more than twenty years, his record completely fails to pass.

In making our judicial assessment we will, to be generous, abandon our usual rule that good things done by his various governments should be attributed to his subordinates, and that only the bad should be attributed to him. Making this noble and generous gesture, what do we find?

In his first period of office, from 1939–1941, he saw that a war was imminent; he re-introduced compulsory military training; he led a united nation into war; he raised the second AIF; he despatched it abroad; after he was out of office, his successors inherited a trained and experienced AIF and used them effectively in New Guinea and the islands; he created a munitions organisation in Australia, appointed Essington Lewis as its Director and helped him to assemble a great team of industrialists which his successors saw no reason to change thereafter; put into production aircraft and weapons of war on schedules which stood the test of time; went to the Middle East and visited our fighting troops as far west as Benghazi; went to Great Britain and brought messages of comfort and encouragement to the bombed people of Britain; visited America and urged the impossibility of neutrality; returned to Australia and created the Department of War Organisation of Industry, whose labours were thereafter essential.

But, with our usual perception, we perceived under this spurious facade the natural indolence of the man. We persevered. We saw the natural frivolity of the man when he devoted a Saturday afternoon to opening, in Sydney, an exhibition of purely representational art.

When we heard of this at the golf-links, we were strengthened in our sense of mission. And we succeeded. He was thanked, over-generously we thought, and relieved of office.

What shall we say of his second long period of office, from 1949 onwards! It would be tedious to re-state our views, for we have made them clear day by day. It is sufficient to say that, while gullible people have been persuaded to believe that the period was one of great expansion and almost turbulent activity, expert minds, such as we have at our command, have always detected the errors and have seen vividly that good results can never be conceded to flow from fallacious reasoning. Industrial peace can never be applauded if our industrial correspondent detects a spirit of appeasement. Equity shareholders cannot be easily deluded into accepting radical measures against inflation. Mr Menzies' quaint belief that government public works to produce light and power and water storage and roads and modern transport were in aid of private enterprise was at all times challenged by us except, of course, and we have always made this concession to the rules of courtesy, on those rare occasions when we had some special interest to serve and therefore relapsed into an occasional period of neutrality.

> Perhaps the late statesman's greatest error was his obstinate refusal to recognise that the 'fourth estate', if we may recall that immortal phrase, is the real ruler of the nation. Being of a reactionary and fundamentally uneducated mind, he retained an atavistic belief that political power belongs to elected persons and not to those chosen by Providence to be newspaper proprietors. This was a fatal error. No adroitness in debate could conceal it. We trust that now he has gone, and the shoddy magic of his vulgar eloquence has gone with him, the nation will return to our fold and realise that we remain willing to offer guidance, informed by study and skill, untainted by personal interests, to a people whose feelings at today's news must be those of men and women who have come out of the 'shades of the prison-house' and can once more live in a state of guided freedom.

One year, returning from an exhausting overseas trip, my father followed the advice of Ray Maley and sent ahead a message that he would not speak to the press on arrival, but would have a conference the following morning. Nevertheless, on arrival in Sydney there was a large gathering of reporters. He more or less brushed them aside, saying, 'See you tomorrow at ten o'clock.'

As he was making his way out, a young man approached

him. 'Prime Minister, I'm from *The Sydney Morning Herald* . . .' he began.

My father patted him on the shoulder and said, 'That, dear boy, is *your* misfortune.'

It was a good example of his belief that it was not necessary to answer every question that was put to him. It didn't mean that he hated the questioner.

There was considerable consternation in the office of the *Launceston Examiner* one year, before he was due to arrive in that city. The newsmen wanted to ask a certain question that they knew would be unpopular, so they more or less drew straws. The loser was a young cadet reporter who, with a sinking heart, went out to the airport. Bravely he asked the question. Unsurprisingly he got some answer like 'No comment'.

Later, the young man was standing on the footpath when the PM got into his car. My father (referred to as the 'Big B' by my informant) looked up, recognised him, wound down the window and asked, 'How are you getting back into town? Hop in and I'll give you a lift.' He chatted with the young reporter all the way, in a very friendly manner, but of course there was never a word about THE subject.

Another journalist who drew the short straw was Frank Harvey, who was sent to Perth airport with the warning that he wouldn't get very far. Clearly a man of ingenuity, he handed a note to one of the PM's staff. It read:

> Dear Prime Minister,
>
> I am a recently arrived English journalist working for *The West Australian*. My Australian colleagues tell me that you do not normally grant interviews to the press.
>
> However, I would be immensely glad if we could share a couple of minutes of your time to chat about (a) cricket (b) tennis or (c) Betty Grable's legs.
>
> Yours sincerely,
>
> Frank Harvey

The note was handed to my father, who roared with laughter, beckoned Harvey over and had a 'chat'.

After the publication in 2011 of my father's letters to me, John Hamilton wrote to me to say he was astonished 'to find on p. 227 the account of "an interview I gave a young man named Hamilton for my birthday"'.

> I still remember the occasion well – myself *petrified* at being sent to interview a figure who had the reputation of not suffering fools – particularly fools from the press – gladly! But instead being utterly charmed by your father, who was

> kindness itself, and gave me a long and happy interview which was widely used around Australia.

Another journalist who felt that Menzies was not quite 'Ming the Merciless' was Wallace Brown, who recalled in his book *Ten Prime Ministers* an encounter with him in Parliament House thus:

> I was leaving my office late at night and going down the stairs to the corridor leading to King's Hall. Out of the Prime Minister's suite in the corner of the building came first White (Parliamentary Librarian and National Librarian), rapidly and alone, and about twenty paces behind him and slowly, Menzies and Holt.
>
> Menzies turned and nodded in recognition as I walked several paces behind and the P.M. and his Treasurer continued on their way. Said Menzies to Holt: 'For God's sake, Harold, give him his bloody library and get him off my back!' As White continued on into the night through King's Hall, Menzies and Holt turned into Holt's office (possibly for a nightcap!), and as I walked past, Menzies nodded to me again, said nothing and winked. I wrote a story next day on an expected Government decision to build a national library. Such was the beauty of that small,

cramped, uncomfortable, democratic and efficient Old Parliament House!

Perhaps surprisingly, my father had good personal relations with Hugh McClure Smith of *The Sydney Morning Herald*. Hugh's daughter Katie asked him to contribute to her autograph book, in which everyone was asked to draw a picture. He wrote:

I am no artist; No! not I
I cannot draw, and do not try.
Under the editorial eye
I'd peak and pine and fade and die
If Hugh should in this book descry
Something that looked like 'printer's pie'.
And so, dear KATE, you should apply
To a more responsive sort of guy!

This was signed and accompanied by a drawing of his face. Not long afterwards he received this verse from Hugh, on *The Sydney Morning Herald* letterhead:

Dear Bob,

How nice of you to find the time
To send my daughter that gay rhyme.
She will, I know, be quite enthralled

Though I am just a bit appalled
That you should think and write of me
As one so lost to charity
That what you call my editorial
Eye would simply be censorial
Were you to try to be pictorial.

Besides, how could I take the part
Of those who practise *Modern* Art,
And then deny to you possession
Of freedom in your self-expression,
However strange the form it took
In dignifying Katherine's book?

Yours ever
Hugh

Geoffrey Syme of the Melbourne *Age* was a great friend, confidant and mentor. The Symes lived within walking distance of our house, and my father was a frequent visitor. They spent many hours in deep discussion, particularly in the 1940s, when my father was gathering groups together to form the Liberal Party.

My father and mother were on very good terms with Frank Packer of the *Daily Telegraph* (Sydney), and his wife, Gretel. In 1962 Frank named his first yacht *Gretel*, and my mother launched it with enthusiasm. She presented the ship with a clock and a barometer. The clock was to enable the crew 'always to know the time in which it won the race' – the race being the America's Cup – and the barometer was 'to ensure there was always fair weather to sail by'. Some years later, my father launched Frank's next yacht, *Dame Pattie*, which also competed in the America's Cup, with my parents there to cheer her on at Newport, Rhode Island.

A good indication of the considerable camaraderie between 'Pig Iron Bob' and the gentlemen of the press, and of the respect in which they held him as early as 1952, is that they gave him a dinner that year. It must have been a light-hearted occasion, because they presented him with an elaborate, illustrated, certificate to 'Robert Gorgeous Menzies'.

In November 1946 he was the guest speaker at an Australian Journalists' Association dinner at the Hotel Canberra. Being in opposition at the time, presumably he had more time to compose a poetic 'masterpiece' as his speech. Here are a few of the verses:

ODE
All hail, great CHIFLEY, whom six States obey
Who sometimes baccy takes and sometimes tea.
Fresh from the battle over Bretton Woods;

Fresh from the brawl on Rosie Kelly's goods;
Fresh from the Caucus and the ALP;
Fresh from launching RIORDAN on the deep blue sea.

How are the boys, my placid Benedict?
Is it still true that JACK LANG has them tricked?
Is BERT behaving? or are Paraguay
And Chile cooking up a breakaway?

And so I toast the monstrous AJA
Who owe their prestige and their noble pay
to Isaac Isaacs and to Ming R. G.
Whose names are reverenced in the Gallery:
I often sit below at Question Time
And gaze aloft at that salubrious clime
Where dwell the journalists in their array
Both blind and deaf to everything I say.

'God bless the press,' I say with Highland piety
It gives to fact an infinite variety.

A word just here about the ABC
That body that has failed most dismally
To give full time to Cricket, but pretends
Jockeys and Starters, Scratchings, Dividends
And puerile programmes to sub-normal brats
Are more important than cricket bats.

So Gentles all, our Legislators
I give the toast of our co-operators
To greet these ever-present hornets
A roll of drums: a silver peal of cornets:
Blow on the sackbut and the violincello;
Lift up your voices with 'New England' bellow:
The AJA, our daily friends and foes.
Up goes the glass, and down the nectar flows.

•

Stewart Cockburn has written that: 'In due course, Menzies mastered television with consummate ease and success. But in doing so, he deferred less than any of his colleagues to TV's constraints. He remained himself, his own man.'

But he did need a little training. When he arrived at the studio for his first television broadcast, he sat in the designated chair. All the lights were turned on. He looked up and demanded that the lights should be turned off. The poor man in charge summoned up all his courage and explained that if they did as he asked he would appear on the screen looking like the bushranger/criminal that some people thought he was. After what was an almost interminable pause, my father relented and agreed to leave the lights on.

Once adjusted, my father took television in his stride and usually appeared to be quite relaxed. He was certainly not distracted when he was interviewed by Robin Day in London. Day, perhaps intolerant of the Menzies pause, kept interrupting. Eventually, my father paused – even longer than usual – then held up his hand and said in a chilly tone, 'Do you mind?' and continued with his answer.

It was such a success that, for days afterwards, people stopped him and said, 'That was wonderful. You got the better of him.'

His last television appearance was filmed at home not long before he died. The room was filled with all the people usually associated with that sort of event, and the devoted Sister Peters, who had bossily and with great good humour nursed him at home for some time, watching from the back. She described it to me:

> TV: Sir Robert, we'll have a rehearsal now.
>
> RGM: I never have a rehearsal.
>
> TV: But we must. You have to speak for exactly the right amount of time.
>
> RGM: How long do you want me to speak?
>
> TV: Four and a half minutes.
>
> RGM: Very well. But no rehearsal.

'He spoke for precisely the correct length of time,' she told me. 'The crew was astonished. They said they had never seen a performance to compare with it.'

A significant indication of how deeply his success as prime minister was felt and resented in some quarters was the unremitting criticisms that were made of him in some parts of the media in the years following his retirement. It was almost a process of demonisation. For years after he had died, the ABC, in particular, seemed to go out of its way to misrepresent him.

I don't think he would have been surprised by this. There is a record of his talking to Churchill after the latter had retired, and Churchill telling my father sadly about the similar treatment he received in Britain. My father told Churchill that this was to be expected from some of the 'clever young men'. It would pass.

Now, in 2013, over thirty years since my father died, I believe that there is a change in the attitude of the Australian media. Their references to him seem to me to be more frequent and much warmer and more balanced than they used to be. I am pleased to have lived long enough to see it.

Canberra, or Dinner's Off

In Canberra during the 1930s and 1940s, my father, like most other MPs, stayed at hotels. One evening he had been invited to dine at Government House and arranged to go with Artie Fadden. He was all dressed up (in a boiled shirt? — no, black tie I think) and waiting in the foyer of the Hotel Canberra, and was no doubt looking at his watch and pacing to and fro. Time, too, was marching on. Eventually, he went round to Artie's room. Artie appeared with fluff all down the front of his dinner suit and said, 'Oh Bob, I dropped one of my studs on the floor and it went under the bed and I've been trying to find it.'

(That was not unlike Artie's experience at a dinner my father took him to at Gray's Inn in London. On that occasion he was wearing a clip-on black tie, which popped off and fell in his soup. Unperturbed, good old Artie just plucked it out and wiped it and put it back in place.)

One night, the train from Melbourne was late getting in to Canberra and my father arrived at the hotel at seven p.m., hoping for some dinner. No. Dinner was off at six-thirty. There could be no breaking the rules. The staff were unimpressed by the fact that he had been staying there for years, and was Leader of the Opposition at the time, and was hungry.

It is hardly surprising that my father shared the view of most MPs: Canberra was rather a bleak place that took them away from their families. Of course, his attitude started to change when he lived at The Lodge and it became his only home. But the big revolution came in 1956.

Peter and I were living in Djakarta at the time, and I came back to have a baby. I stayed at The Lodge with my parents. Every night, when my father came home for dinner, he would be lectured by either my mother or me. We pointed out Canberra's failings.

'Bob, *you* try pushing a pram round these awful footpaths.'

'Dad, it's almost impossible to find somewhere to live here.'

On and on we went. In the end, he said: 'Well, we're stuck with Canberra, whether we like it or not, so we might as well do it properly.'

Great credit must be given to Ken Herde, a senior officer in the Prime Minister's Department. He was a practical man who had a flair for organising. He and my father used to see each other on a regular basis to discuss departmental business. The Herdes lived in the same neighbourhood so it was easy for Ken to call in on his way home. In the relaxed atmosphere of The Lodge, the discussions naturally widened to include the future of Canberra as the national capital.

In his memoires of this time, Ken wrote:

> Mr Menzies was very interested in my views and we seemed to share the same ideas. In this way we had quite a few such talks. In due course, prior to him going to London for a Commonwealth Prime Ministers' meeting in 1956, he asked me to prepare a paper on the problems I saw, together with ideas on how they could be resolved so that Canberra's future planning and development could be corrected.

Ken wrote the paper while my father was away, as he went on to relate:

> When the Prime Minister returned I gave it to him and at the same time a copy to Allen Brown [Secretary of the PM's Department] . . . A couple of days later he told me that the Prime Minister agreed with it and would be putting it before the next Cabinet meeting to get their endorsement. Cabinet agreed with all the proposals and the Minister for the Interior (who had responsibility for Canberra) was instructed to prepare appropriate legislation.

After overcoming some objections from the minister, who did not want to lose control of Canberra, the legislation prepared by Ken was adopted and the National Capital Development Commission (the name suggested by him) was set up. Walter Burley Griffin's original plans for the city were dusted off and the lake was put in.

John Overall was put in charge of the newly created NCDC and there was *action*. My father claimed that when Cabinet made a decision about Canberra, Mr (later Sir John) Overall would have the bulldozers on the spot at the crack of dawn next morning.

Sir John Overall ran the NCDC for fourteen years, 1958 to 1973. In 1963 his task was made much easier by the appointment of a young Country Party MP, Doug Anthony, as Minister for the Interior. Previous ministers hadn't taken much interest in Canberra. Doug (my father always called

Robert Gordon Menzies at school in Jeparit (second from left).

The drawing my father did when he was at Wesley in 1911. 'Sunset and Evening Star' (Tennyson).

My Father's family (left to right): Mother, Belle, Syd, Father, Bob, Frank, Les.

The plaque on the Post Office in Penzance.

My grandfather handing 'How to Vote' cards to my parents outside Trinity Grammar School, Kew.

Mama ready to be presented at Court.

Me with my teeth painted in.

The 1st prize winner (Mama dressed as a swaggie) is chosen. My father laughing in the background.

The Queen investing my mother with the G.B.E.

The last Christmas at The Lodge, 1965. Back row (left to right): Ken, Sibby, me, Peter, Marjorie, Alec, Ian. Front and middle row: Diana, Trini, Geoffrey, Mama, Edwina, Donald, Papa, Robert, Lindsay, Penny.

Dad and his sister Belle hamming it up for the camera.

My brother Ian (Parker).

The gang arriving at London Airport for the coronation. Left to right: my mother, my father, me, Stewart Cockburn, Hazel Craig and Sir Thomas White (our High Commissioner in London).

Walking up the steps of Parliament House.

Mama and Papa with our daughter Edwina.

Peter, me, Mama and Papa, with a friend at Walmer.

My parents arriving in London, being greeted by (left to right) Sibby, Penny, Dwina, Trini.

My mother planting a ceremonial tree with her usual enthusiasm.

him Douglas) brought a new approach. He and his wife Margot rented and later bought a house there and sent their children to the local school. They quickly became part of the community.

It is of great significance to me that Doug wrote recently for an article in the *Canberra Times*: 'Many of the problems and concerns of the Canberra people drifted into the hands of the Prime Minister and his wife Dame Pattie.' He went on, 'Canberrans needed someone to whom they could voice opinions and their complaints. I soon learned that it was politic to keep a good relationship with Dame Pattie who was very concerned with many of the problems facing the people of Canberra. Keeping her informed was very useful in my relationship with the Prime Minister.' What more compelling evidence could you find that both my parents had a deep concern for Canberra?

Canberra would not be the city it is today if Cabinet, persuaded by my father, had not endorsed Ken Herde's submission. It was not until 2006, fifty years later, that his contribution was recognised tangibly, and R.G. Menzies Walk was opened on the north side of the lake. It could not be a more appropriate memorial. It is next to *his* lake, it looks across to *his* Parliament House, it is in the capital city of *his* country, and – as a bonus – he enjoyed walking.

In 2012 an admirable addition was made: a statue, by Peter Corlett, of my father walking next to his lake. Alongside the walk there are four plaques with photos and stories about Menzies, the man who has been rightly credited with starting Canberra on the way to becoming the city it is today. One of these reads:

> Menzies' contribution to the renewed city went well beyond the establishment of the NCDC. He and Dame Pattie Menzies made The Lodge their home, Deakin and Forrest their neighbourhood, and Canberra their city. Motivated by his irrepressible enthusiasm for cricket, in October 1951 Menzies inaugurated the annual Prime Minister's XI cricket match at Manuka Oval – against the visiting international touring team that year, the West Indies.
>
> In his memoirs, *The Measure of the Years* (1970), Menzies recalled his affection for Canberra simply: 'my dream had been given shape . . .'

The Lodge

Before I was born in 1928, my parents bought a house in Kew, Melbourne, and it was their home for over twenty years. (Peter and I are now the proud possessors of the hand-push lawnmower that went with the house. We still use it. To be accurate, Peter uses it.) When my father became PM in 1939, my parents retained the house in Melbourne, where they lived part-time, and moved into The Lodge.

In 1927 the plans for The Lodge had been approved and building was to proceed while the Prime Minister Mr Bruce and his wife were overseas. But never reckon without Treasury. I have been told they proclaimed that the house was too big and expensive, so someone had the bright idea that the simplest thing would be to chop a few feet off the front, thereby making the sitting room and dining room smaller. The result was that only ten people could be seated comfortably.

Very good furniture had been made, but the dining room chairs were extra wide, which added to the difficulty. Incidentally, those chairs were carved on the back with 'P.M.', which inspired my mother to claim they were hers, with her initials!

The previous incumbents had been the Lyons, a large family. The main part of the house had four bedrooms and two dressing rooms, one of which was suitable for use as a bedroom. This had not really been adequate for them so they had converted the area at the top of the stairs plus a small outside balcony into a sort of dormitory for the children.

Naturally there was a certain amount of wear and tear over the years. My mother felt it was up to her to organise some redecoration, and to this end Mrs Dolly Guy Smith from Myer in Melbourne was employed. Mrs Guy Smith was not one to spend money frivolously, so she and my mother suited each other admirably. Damaged carpets were cut to fit smaller rooms, curtains were adjusted similarly, new loose covers were made for chairs and sofas, and walls were painted.

My parents made good use of the billiard room. It was probably my father's greatest relaxation during those two traumatic years at the beginning of the war. When he came home for lunch, he and my mother played a game of snooker, and again at night after dinner before he went back to work. My mother claimed that if she won she knew there was a crisis on. (She was too modest – she played very well.)

They had the good fortune to get to know the master of billiards, Walter Lindrum. That marvellous man, always so unassuming, raised huge sums of money for the war effort, and also taught my parents the finer points of the game – well, he tried. They were both good pupils.

By the late 1940s my brother Ken was married and my brother Ian (known as Parker) was living in the country, so the house in Kew was too big. My parents sold it and moved to a smaller one, which, as it turned out, didn't really suit them. With no regrets, they sold that when they moved back into The Lodge in 1949. At the time, they had no idea that it would be their only home for the next sixteen years.

My father displayed carefully contrived incompetence in the domestic sphere. He always managed to look awkward with a tea towel in his hand; I assumed he had no idea what it was for. But his cover was blown when my beloved Aunty Belle (also known to us as Belinski) told me that she and my father had washed up every night when they were living with their Scottish grandmother in Ballarat. They were always critical of Grandma's propensity for keeping ancient, cracked, and smelly dishes. One night, as one was washing and the other drying, they looked at each other surreptitiously, made sure no-one could see, and dropped one of the offending plates on the floor. It smashed satisfactorily into many pieces. No doubt that would have been worth two chapters of the Bible.

When my parents were first married, they invited some friends for a meal, and my mother cooked what was rather special in those days: a chicken. She brought it to the table and, like a dutiful wife, said, 'You carve, Bob.' So my father picked up the knife and fork, went *clunk, clunk* and cut it into four. My mother, appalled, muttered, 'That has to go around six people. Give me the knife.' (Lady Macbeth?) From that day on she always carved, and with great expertise. The moral of the story is that if you don't want to do something make sure you make a hash of it. My mother advised me, 'Never learn to milk a cow or you'll have to do it.'

One night at The Lodge my mother was standing at the sideboard carving the roast beef. In came a nervous and shaking parlourmaid, Violet. 'Madam,' she said, 'there's a man in the kitchen.'

Without hesitation, Madam, still holding – or perhaps 'brandishing' would be a better word – the carving knife, walked into the kitchen. The man took one look at the knife and the little lady wielding it, and ran out the back door. Whereupon Madam walked over to the door, an ordinary wooden and wire door, snibbed it and said, 'I've told you before to keep that door snibbed.' Of course, anyone could have broken in easily. In these days of high security such a situation is almost unimaginable.

That was the only time I can remember someone breaking into the house, but the garden was a different matter. The fence around the garden consisted of a couple of wires between posts, and the gates were rarely closed. There was no security. People often wandered in, and tourists in buses stopped to look: 'There's the PM and Mrs Menzies having a cup of coffee . . .' That problem was solved by arranging large pot plants to block the view.

One night my mother drove my father back to the office after dinner. Just outside the gate there was a car with a few people standing next to it in the pouring rain. My mother thought, 'Poor things, I'll stop and help them when I get back.' But when she got back they and the car had disappeared. The next morning all was revealed: they had driven in, down the bank and all over the croquet lawn. The poor gardeners spent hours restoring it.

Within a week there was another nocturnal visitor: a horse. That provided another day's work.

There were other hazards and uninvited guests: hornets. My mother reacted badly to insect stings, so she rang the relevant department to ask them to arrange for their removal.

Time passed.

Nothing happened.

Eventually it did. She was bitten on the face, and within seconds looked as if she had mumps. She wrapped a scarf around her head, got into her car and drove to the department. She walked in, removed the scarf, and said, '*Now* will you do something about those hornets?'

I can't leave the subject of insects without mentioning the unveiling of the Australian-American War Memorial by the Queen in 1954. I was sitting next to my mother, and without the slightest change in her demeanour she begged me to squash an insect that had gone down her back – 'No . . . further to the right . . . up more . . . no, near the middle' – with me desperately trying to find the offender, at the same time trying to look sedate and interested in proceedings. When we got back to The Lodge, she uncharacteristically stripped (partially): her back was covered with big red weals. She had the most remarkable stoicism and self-control.

My mother also took exception to another form of wildlife: currawongs. My parents used to sit outside and have a drink (Vegemite glasses were favourites for this purpose) or a cup of coffee or tea. My mother kept a shanghai tucked into the wisteria nearby. From time to time she would leap to her feet, grab it and take a pot-shot at the currawongs, saying, 'I can't stand those beastly creatures – they're always killing the baby birds.'

One day my father said, weakly: 'Pat, for goodness' sake, sit down. One day you're going to hit a passing pedestrian and then we'll be in *real* trouble.'

Those who remember The Lodge in those days will know that there was not a hope of hitting a passing pedestrian.

My mother loved gardens and gardening. During the war she had grown lots of vegetables in our Melbourne garden, so she was rather surprised to find that there was no vegetable garden at The Lodge. That state of affairs was quickly rectified, and a suitable garden was created and flourished and became bountiful – so much so that she did lots of bottling and, later, freezing.

Some of the former secretaries from Parliament House still talk about how, when the big black car arrived, the driver would sometimes come in with a basket of vegetables and say, 'Dame Pattie said you girls don't have time to feed yourselves properly.'

The next additions to the garden were chooks, then ducks.

There was a bit of drama one year because a local pack of dogs got in and killed the ducks, which, possibly, were meant for Christmas dinner. The police – the Federal Police, no less – went around the neighbourhood trying to identify the dogs. (I have been assured by the neighbours that this is a true story.) The Canadian diplomats in nearby Daly Crescent claimed diplomatic immunity. However, the owners of the dogs got together and drove – in the *Canadians'* car – to Wagga to buy replacement ducks which they presented to my mother.

So The Lodge was very much part of the neighbourhood. If children kicked their balls into the garden they could easily nick through the useless wire fence and retrieve them. The Fishers, who lived near the back gate, often drove through because it was a short cut. In fact, the Fishers' young son, Bill, rang the bell one day and my mother went to the door.

Dame P: 'Hello, Bill, what do you want?'

Bill: 'I'm doing a project at school and want to ask Mr Menzies some questions.'

Dame P: 'We're having lunch, but come in.'

With great composure Bill came in and sat at the table, opened his exercise book, licked his pencil, asked his questions and wrote down my father's answers. Having got what he wanted, he very politely said thank you and went home to his stunned parents.

Perhaps his parents were used to being stunned. In 1954, when the Queen came to Canberra, there was a grand occasion at the front of Parliament House. My mother, with other dignitaries, was sitting there. Amongst the masses was the Fisher family. Bill, aged about seven, spotted his friend Dame Pattie, pushed through the crowd and sat on her knee throughout the whole parade.

Children were very much in evidence during my parents' time at The Lodge. My mother often used to look after some of my four children there during the years we were back in Canberra from overseas posts. I was one of very few young wives to have that sort of grandparental support. Looking back, I can see I took advantage – presumptuously – of being able to drop a child off and say, 'Can I leave her here for half an hour while I go to the shops?' If my mother wasn't there the cook, Mrs Nesbitt, would entertain or tolerate the little pet in the kitchen. Oh, what a charmed life I have led!

My mother often used to have some or all of my brother's six children to stay – on at least one occasion with their dog. Ken's daughter Diana has fond memories of staying there with the granny she loved so much:

> We had great times at The Lodge when we were little. Granny would take us out for long days at the river and then at night we would be allowed to have our choice of tinned spaghetti or baked beans or tinned sausages and beans as a treat while we watched *Disneyland*. The only

problem was that the labels all came off in the boiling water! I also remember having chickenpox and being very upset about not being able to be involved in Guy Fawkes night. Granny arranged to have the big bonfire under my window so that I could see without infecting everyone.

With the exception of red meat, The Lodge seemed to be quite self-sufficient. I remember the vegetable garden, the chickens (with heads on and off), the flowers, learning how to ride a boys' bike down the grass slope (and falling onto the central bar). I remember the big laundry copper, the kitchen, Granny's preserved fruit . . . she got involved in everything. I remember helping Violet prepare Grandpa's breakfast tray with half a grapefruit and boiled eggs and toast. There was also a piano outside their room which we 'played' often. It must have driven him mad, and he said so but we weren't daunted.

Regardless of the children, official entertainments like dinner parties were still maintained. I like to think that The Lodge was so obviously a family house that it added to the character and relaxed atmosphere of these occasions.

The vital area, of course, was the kitchen. It was, with the possible exception of the billiard room, the largest room in the house. (Unlike the sitting room and dining room, it had not been cut back in size by Treasury.) It must have been a nightmare to work in. One cook claimed it was like a route march from the stove to the sink to the fridge. My mother knew it well, and in the early days often did the cooking herself. But my mother's natural frugality, combined with her reluctance to spend public money, meant that any alterations were piecemeal.

The sink with a wooden draining board was replaced with stainless steel. My mother asked the carpenter what he was going to do with the old draining board. She was dismayed when he replied 'Throw it away', so she kept a large piece. I have it today: an antique, historic, chopping board.

The old fuel stove was replaced by an oil-fired Aga. One Sunday, with a dinner party that night, the Aga died. My mother rang the company but of course no one was working at the weekend. So the man who owned the local franchise, Jim Fitzhardinge, came. He claims he knew no more than my mother, and it ended up with them both lying on the floor and peering into the innards of the monster. Happily, they were successful – it was in the days before takeaway.

Sometimes food for these dinner parties came from unexpected sources. For years the land behind The Lodge was vacant. In the season it was a good source of mushrooms. My mother and her neighbours would go out with their baskets, collecting.

Things in the kitchen were easier when the competent and congenial Heather Nesbitt became the cook. She had a four-year-old daughter, and they became a bit like part of the family. Mrs Nesbitt, who was also pretty good at dressmaking, even made me a garment to wear when I was pregnant. Some years later, she married my father's widowed driver, Alf Stafford, and their wedding reception was held at The Lodge.

Because the kitchen was so large, my mother decided it would be the ideal venue for a fancy-dress party for me and my friends. My main memory of the evening is of my father sitting, Buddha-like, draped in a sheet, with a red ribbon tied around his exceptionally large tummy, and a notice: 'THE INFLATION PROBLEM'.

My mother was keen on fancy-dress parties, and happily spent hours inventing and creating strange creations to wear to them. Her most brilliant piece of acting and dressing-up took place when she and my father were travelling on board the ship *Orcades*. A fellow passenger has told me that a little swaggie emerged and wandered in and out through all the pirates and others, looking for a place to boil his billy. He had a dirty face, a hat with corks, baggy old trousers, a swag on his back and a billy. He sat on the floor and produced twigs and set a fire to boil the billy. No one could work out who it was, until my mother was presented with the first prize.

•

Back to The Lodge: the dining room was supplied with a bell which rang in the kitchen. It took the form of a small brass plate set into the carpet at the kitchen end of the table. My mother liked to sit at the other end so she could 'see what was going on', so she asked for a bell at her end too. A small knob was set into the table and attached to a wire, which went under and to the middle of the table. From there it seemed to be tied up with string, and then went straight down through a hole in the carpet and was connected to the kitchen. And if that sounds like a Heath Robinson arrangement, it was.

One night, with ten people at the table, my father started telling a story, and accidentally put his foot on the bell. Violet came in and asked him to take his foot off it. But it went on and on even after the offending foot was removed – we could all hear it. Eventually one of the guests, Mick Shann, pushed back his chair and got under the table and pulled out the wires. 'That's fixed it.' Mick could get away with a lot, partly because his father had taught my father English, and partly because of his own personality and humour.

A particularly vivid memory is the visit of Lord Swinton, the British Minister for Commonwealth Relations. Loud – no, stentorian – bellowing came from under the stairs: 'John,

John! Morrison, Morrison! Here am I, locked in the lavatory, and I'm supposed to be at Parliament House at ten o'clock. John, John! Morrison! Morrison!' My mother's remedy was not unlike the bell arrangement: she put some tape over the lock so it couldn't be used or get stuck. (For the record, John Morrison, Lord Swinton's aide, became the second Lord Dunrossil.)

By the mid-1950s it had been decided that something should be done about the shortage of entertainment space at The Lodge. So, no more snooker. The big table, which was also used for displaying Christmas cards and our wedding presents, was taken away and the room was turned into another sitting room.

•

For much of his life my father was a great walker. He walked confidently around city streets, day or night. On one occasion I was with my parents in New York and we went to see the musical *Guys and Dolls*. At interval my father said, 'I can't understand a word they're saying. I'm going back to the pub.' (He always referred to any hotel, however grand, as a 'pub', with the exception of the Savoy in London, which was 'the Saveloy'.) So off he went, walking.

At the end of the performance, the man assigned by the American authorities to protect him appeared and asked,

'Where's the Prime Minister?' The poor man was horrified to hear that the VIP he was supposed to be protecting had walked home at half time.

In London, too, I regret to say, that same VIP used to gain his freedom by going out the side door of the Saveloy and walking along the embankment to escape his 'minders'.

With this attitude to personal security, my parents were somewhat bemused to be told in the 1950s that it had been decided to build a guard house at the front gate of The Lodge, and to install a guard. The fence was still merely a two strand wire job. My brother Ken managed to suppress his ambition to put on a false beard and rush in with a smoking bomb yelling, 'Death to Menzies!' All very funny then; not so these days.

In fact, it would have been impossible for one man to protect that place at night, so who could blame the guards if they didn't always take it seriously?

When young Wendy Johnson was staying with my mother, one night she heard: 'Wendy, come here. Look out the window. What is that patch of blue? I know we haven't got a plumbago bush there . . .'

'No, Dame Pattie, that's a man in a blue shirt, lying on the ground.'

My mother was sure it must be the security guard, who might have had a heart attack, so she rushed downstairs to go outside. Wendy couldn't stop her, but ran to the phone and rang her policeman neighbour, Ray Whitrod, who said, 'Don't let her go out – bring her in!' He immediately drove round.

It turned out to be the security guard, but he hadn't had a heart attack, just too much whisky.

•

No memories of mine can ignore a young woman who worked at The Lodge for about ten years. Agnes was a Ukrainian girl who had set off to go to university just as the Nazis took over her country. Her war became traumatic and terrifying, and she found herself alone or with strangers.

Sticks stolen from the forest at night – a risky enterprise – were needed to make fires to cook and keep warm. After some time someone took pity on her and employed her in a kitchen where she acquired cooking skills and, more importantly, survived.

She met and married a Pole, Wasyl Glembowski, and after the war they migrated to Australia. At that time, those in control of employment for migrants often sent husbands and wives to different towns or even different states. Agnes was selected for a job at The Lodge, which gave her the 'status' to enable Wasyl to go to Canberra too.

So to Canberra they went, on a slow and unheated train, which arrived at five a.m. on a cold April day. There was no waiting room at the station, so they sat on a bench outside for several hours until they were collected and driven to The Lodge. Agnes was dropped off there, but neither of them knew where Wasyl was disappearing to in the car. In fact, he was taken to the migrant hostel on nearby Capital Hill.

With considerable generosity of spirit, I shall refrain from naming the housekeeper at The Lodge at the time. But did 'Mrs X' greet the poor, weary traveller in a normal human way? 'Here's your room . . . Would you like a cup of tea?' Not on your nellie! She said: 'There's the washing up.'

This was followed by: 'What's your name?' When the reply was 'Nadezhda' (which translates into English as 'Nadia'), Mrs X said that was much too difficult and they would call her Agnes. It was not until forty years later that I found out that our much loved Ag was not Ag at all. (Yes, I confess: we sinned too, in typical Australian fashion, by abbreviating Agnes to Ag.)

Mr Chifley was the prime minister when Agnes arrived in Canberra, but neither he nor Mrs Chifley had any idea what was going on backstage: that Agnes was at the beck and call of Mrs X and the rest of the domestic staff.

Mrs Chifley rarely came to Canberra. Both she and Agnes felt rather lonely at The Lodge, and so, in spite of Agnes's limited English, they had lots of conversations and came to like each other. For years Mrs Chifley sent Agnes

Christmas cards. They have now been given to Chifley house in Bathurst.

Agnes's life changed dramatically when my parents arrived at The Lodge early in 1950. My mother was surprised to learn that Wasyl was still living at the migrant hostel, and immediately arranged for him to move to The Lodge to be with Agnes. He continued to work elsewhere.

Just before she'd left Germany, Agnes had fallen and, as a result, suffered a miscarriage. She had continuing medical problems. My mother thought she looked thin, and when she heard what had happened, she made an appointment with a GP, drove Agnes there and waited for her outside. The doctor said she needed an operation. The patient didn't like him. So my mother made an appointment with her own specialist in Melbourne.

In due course, Agnes had her first plane trip, accompanying my parents in the VIP plane. As she was leaving to go to the doctor, my mother handed her a packet of sandwiches, saying, 'You might get hungry if you have to wait a long time.' Following instructions from the specialist, the operation took place in Canberra, and my mother visited Agnes in hospital several times after it was finally performed.

But . . . cast your bread on the waters . . .

Not long after moving into The Lodge, our old dog, Ming, a white Pekingese, died. Some time later, when my parents were away overseas, Agnes, with limited resources, including the language, managed to find a replacement – almost a replica of Ming – in Yass. She presented the new dog to my mother on her return.

From time to time overseas guests stayed at The Lodge. Agnes always asked if they had any washing to be done. One man said, 'No, no, no' – until the night before he left. Then he said, 'Oh, well, actually, yes.' He handed over twenty-seven shirts. (That cannot possibly be accurate, but it's her version of the story.)

This was well before the days of drying machines, but the washing machine did its job. Agnes and the prime minister's wife – contrary to the public perception of how she filled in her time – sat up for hours drying shirts in front of the Aga, ironing and sewing on buttons.

One visiting distinguished American stayed at The Lodge and had an afternoon sleep. Agnes had instructions to wake him at six so he could be ready for dinner at the American Embassy. When the time came to leave for the dinner, my father was pacing up and down in the front hall and looking at his watch. Eventually, he asked, 'Ag, did you wake him?'

Her reply was: 'Yes. But what does "Hmmm" mean in American?'

My father was very much amused, and of course told his guest, who greeted Ag with 'Hmmm?' when she took in his tea the next morning.

Agnes once said to me, 'I get so cross when people say Menzies was snooty,' sticking her nose in the air. 'He was always making jokes.'

She became fluent in English and typing, and after leaving The Lodge was employed in an office for many years. Most of these stories were told to me by Agnes in 1995. She died in Canberra in 2009.

Kirribilli House

In the 1950s Eric Harrison, as the Member for Wentworth, went to my father and told him about Kirribilli House on the north side of the harbour in Sydney. In 1919, when Billy Hughes was PM, it had been acquired by the government because it was believed it could be useful as a defence against the Russians. After that, it had languished, been used as a boarding house for many years, and it was now run-down. The question was: should it be sold or used for some other purpose?

It is a pleasant-looking house with a spectacular view across the garden to the harbour, the Sydney Harbour Bridge, and the city beyond.

Harrison and Menzies decided to set it up with the primary purpose of creating an official guesthouse for VIP visitors from overseas, along the lines of Blair House in Washington. They did not establish it as a prime ministerial residence in Sydney. They did, however, make provision for the house to be used by the prime minister when it was not being used otherwise.

It was agreed that the 'heavy hand of Government' would spoil the proposed restoration, so, although Ken Herde from the PM's Department was put in charge of overseeing everything, all the work was carried out by private enterprise.

The architect, John Mansfield, renowned for his restoration work, was engaged for the project. The interior decoration and furnishing was put in the hands of Helen Blaxland (later Dame Helen), who was known for having special skills in that field. Showing considerable patriotism, she did all of that work in an honorary capacity.

When the renovations had been completed and Mr and Mrs Ferry had been installed to run the place, a 'practice' weekend was held. My parents stayed there, and those who had worked to bring it all together were invited to dinner. It was declared to be a great success.

The Japanese PM, Mr Nobusuke Kishi, was one of the first visitors, and then came the British PM, Mr Harold Macmillan. They both expressed their delight at staying there. The purpose of the house was being fulfilled and a significant contribution was being made to the success of high-level visits from overseas.

One person whose impressions of Sydney were vastly improved was my father. He had previously stayed at Ushers Hotel and, when that went out of business, the Hotel Australia. Treasurer Artie Fadden's comment was, 'The only high-class thing there is the tariff.'

It was not until after my father had retired that prime ministers – of both political persuasions – began to regard Kirribilli House solely as a residence for prime ministers. This is not in accord with the original intention, and I regret it. I regret also that we now have no official guesthouse for foreign dignitaries.

The Best Country in the World: Australia

At the beginning of the 1914–18 war my grandparents held a family conference. That was their normal method of dealing with matters of importance. The decision they made was to have far-reaching consequences for my father's future.

It was decided that Les and Frank would join up and go to the war, while Bob would stay home and study and be there for his parents. I have been told that many families at that time made the same decision when they had more than one son: one stayed home. Bob was naturally upset, but it was the family's decision and he felt bound to accept it.

In 1939 his mother said publicly: 'We told him again and again that two sons from a family was as much and more than a country expected . . . We needed someone at home to look after us. It was a difficult decision, and I think that is why he was perhaps the bravest of all my boys.'

In the course of his life in politics, Bob was often taunted about not having gone to the war. He didn't feel able to reply, but it hurt. In the long run, I believe he did infinitely more for his country than he would have as a soldier. He once said to his sister, Belle, 'I was not able to go to the war, so I will devote my life to Australia.'

It has also been said and written that my father desperately wanted to live in Britain and go into politics there. I am unaware of any evidence for this whatsoever.

That is not to say he didn't love Britain. Like all Australian schoolchildren he learnt British history and read English literature. They were his favourite subjects. So it is easy to understand his reactions when he first went to England in 1935. The future Lord Warden of the Cinque Ports wrote in his diary:

> . . . a fair sea and a bright sun and the channel ferry has us in Dover Harbour in 55 minutes. As we enter we have the White Cliffs on our right, and crowning them the Dover Castle. At last we are in England . . . our minds

> abandoned to those reflections which can so strangely move the souls of those who go 'home' to a land they have never seen . . .
>
> Enter the great hall of William Rufus and find on the floor a brass plate marking where Warren Hastings stood his trial nearly 150 years ago. Stand beside it recapturing the great description by Macauley and listen for ringing tones of Burke's great denunciation. For the moment almost imagine I *am* Hastings . . . until I remember that his person was small and emaciated, and realise I am not cast for the part. But the Hall . . . stirs up unforgettable emotions.

I suspect that many of those emotions were with him when he spoke in that same place some years later.

He also wrote about a meeting at 10 Downing Street, another famous place that later became familiar to him:

> Cabinet room with Robert Walpole looking down from the mantelpiece . . . in this room have sat and presided Walpole, Chatham, Pitt, Disraeli, Gladstone, Lloyd George. If only walls could speak!

Later:

> We call at Milton's cottage at Chalfont St Giles, where, in a tiny low ceilinged room, he wrote a great part of Paradise Lost.

And still later:

> First visit to Chequers in Buckinghamshire. A wonderful day passing through Windsor (where we pass the Castle and Eton, and before that the riverside green fields of Runnymede) . . . [At Chequers] there is a stained glass window inscribed: 'This house of peace and ancient memories was given to England as a thanksgiving for her deliverance in the Great War 1914–18 as a place of rest and recreation for her Prime Ministers forever.'
>
> The whole thing is a striking epitome of the English regard for the Parliamentary Institution.
>
> Half a mile from the house, on a point of the Chilterns, we look around country rather like that around Kyneton; it is the very heart of English history. 'The Roman road to Wendover . . .' is just below us. Between it and us are the grassy excavations of the old camp from which the Britons defended themselves against the Roman invaders . . . Walk up the drive along which nearly 300 years ago, the dead body of John Hampden was carried by his Roundheads to the chant of the 90th psalm. The Great House and the

> church are practically as they were in Hampden's day and they would stir the soul of an Australian Trade Union Secretary.
>
> What a day! I have literally been in the presence of the Great Charter among the barons assembled at Runnymede; I have seen the very handwriting of the man whose sword and mind made England a free country, I have stood where stood many times the great John Hampden, and have sat awhile in the invisible presence of the heart of liberty.

That diary was written during my father's first visit to England. Over the years he went there many times.

In the 1930s he went to London to appear before the Privy Council, accompanied by his junior, K.W. Asprey. They won the case. The Law Lords then approached my father and asked him to stay and join the bar there. They said they would find him rooms in the best chambers in London, and guarantee him a huge income, and in due course find him a safe seat for the House of Commons, if that was what he wanted. His reply was: 'Thank you, gentlemen, but my future lies in Australia.' (This piece of information was passed on to me by Asprey's daughter.)

Over the years several people in Britain urged him to stay and go into politics there. Lady Astor even offered him all her sapphires if he would! As my mother said to me, it was all very flattering, but his answer was always the same. He was Australian and wanted to live and work in his own country.

I recently unearthed this cutting (date and newspaper unknown) on the same subject:

Rumours about Menzies

Canberra is full of rumours about the future of Opposition Leader Menzies, who leaves on a health trip to England after the referendum campaign.

One is that he is to make room for Richard Casey, Federal President of the Liberal Party.

The story is that Menzies can be persuaded to quit the Liberal leadership in Casey's favour by an offer of a seat in the House of Commons, with the prospect of elevation to the House of Lords, and an eventual return to Australia as Governor-General.

A Come-Back

The rumours overlook the fact that there is probably nothing Menzies would sooner have than the Prime Ministership he lost in 1941 by machinations within his own party.

Nor can it be overlooked that it was Menzies who, almost lone-handed, pulled the non-Labor forces out

> of the deepest trough in their history, after the Curtin administration took over from the disintegrating UAP-CP.
>
> Whichever way Menzies' future is decided, one thing is certain – he will decide it himself and has no need to bow to dictation from anyone else.

The subject was raised at a press conference in London in May 1960, when it was suggested that my father wanted to retire to a book-lined cottage in Kent. His reply was: 'I don't know where you people get these yarns from. When I retire, I'm going to retire to the best country in the world: Australia.'

Time Off

One big reason why my father was able to remain sane and cope with the job of being PM was his ability to 'switch off'. He had many interests apart from politics. Guests at The Lodge were not harangued about the latest political drama or triviality unless they asked. There were many other subjects that interested him, and he had a great capacity for listening – a gift or accomplishment which is all too rare.

Art

My father's father was an artist, and painted all his life. So, with the help of those artistic genes, my father had enough knowledge of art to make him observant and interested. Not surprisingly, his interest was focused mainly on what has sometimes rather sneeringly been called 'traditional art'. His taste may have been unfashionable in some modern art quarters, but, as he made clear from time to time, he most admired those artists who could actually draw.

His interest in art extended to an interest in the artists themselves. Several became real friends. The Lindsay family – Daryl, Norman, Ruby and Lionel – were friends of my father from his school days. Lionel was the closest. The first book plate he created for Bob harked back to those early days: a schoolboy fishing. Over many years he wrote marvellous letters to Bob, and they could talk and talk about everything under the sun. I remember Lionel sitting at meal time, talking and not eating, and my mother admonishing him: 'Lionel, for goodness sake finish your dinner!'

'Yes, Pat,' he'd say, but before the next mouthful reached his mouth he was talking again. However, he was never dull or boring.

My father's collection of Lionel's work included all his etchings. He was proud and fond of them. And I have in my possession a drawing by Norman Lindsay, under which the artist wrote: 'Thank you for one of the great compliments that life has given me.' But to what, alas, was he referring?

My father was an enthusiastic member of the Savage Club in Melbourne, and for good reasons. The book the club brought out to celebrate its centenary (after his death) was aptly named *Laughter and the Love of Friends*. The club also has historical links with the Australian art world.

My father rose to become the Chief Savage, a role he relished. One member whose company he particularly enjoyed was Harold Herbert, who also used to spend time with us at our holiday house at Mount Macedon. He was very much at ease with children and showed me, with great patience, how to draw a fish. He also contributed to my autograph book.

Another member was the sculptor Victor Greenhalgh. His busts of my father are much admired and can be seen in several places, including the gardens in Ballarat; in Kew, in his electorate of Kooyong; at Walmer Castle, in Kent; and in the family's possession. The fact that Victor Greenhalgh knew his sitter well no doubt contributed to the quality of his work.

Although it hardly comes under the heading of 'Art', the West Brighton Club also provided a lot of fun in my father's life. Some enduring friendships started there over good food and (mostly) non-political conversation and songs which were frequently new words to old tunes. My father was a member there for many, many years, and for a time was its president too. He is now remembered annually at a combined Savage Club/West Brighton Club dinner.

With no premises of their own, the Melbourne Scots hardly rate as a club, but one of my father's favourite annual events was their St Andrew's Night Dinner. In spite of letting the side down somewhat by not wearing a kilt – 'With my shape I would look ridiculous in a kilt' – he was made president.

The dinner always included a haggis and the Scottish drink Atholl Brose. After the haggis was piped in, my father would rise and give a spirited rendition of Burns' 'Ode to the Haggis'. Then, arm raised, he would clutch his dirk and plunge it into the haggis with great gusto.

When it came to proclaiming the Gaelic words that traditionally accompany that action he did need a little help. I have envelopes on which he has written the phonetic spelling he used for those occasions: 'SHAW TARKUS VREEAH UN ROING HOOSA UN YOIL. HA! SKEE-UN.' He would place the prompt discreetly on the table in front of him, then return it to his pocket.

After that diversion, back to Art . . .

When he was in Sydney my father often dined with Sir James (Jim) McGregor, who would gather at his house about half a dozen congenial men, often artists. One was Will Ashton, another was Charles Lloyd Jones. Sir Charles was better known as the man who ran David Jones successfully for many years, but he was also an extremely talented artist. Those gatherings of real friends were a blessed respite from the pressure and strain of my father's political life, particularly during the war and when he was in opposition.

At other times Sir James included women. During the war, there was clothes rationing and many women developed a nifty trick of making dresses out of curtain or furnishing material, which was not rationed. That was not always a success, as Mrs Owen, wife of the judge William Owen, discovered. She found herself sitting on a sofa covered in the same material as her skirt.

Over the years my father acquired a lot of Australian paintings, some by well known artists, others not. One that he particularly valued – not Australian – was given to him by the artist, Sir Winston Churchill. My father bequeathed it to Parliament House, where it now hangs.

My mother also became the owner of a Churchill painting but in an odd way. My parents were staying with the Churchills at a time when my mother was keen on photography. With all innocence, she said, 'I want to get a picture.'

Winston said, 'Clemmie is getting it for you.'

This response puzzled my mother until Clemmie appeared with one of Winston's paintings, which she then presented to her. Years later my mother gave it to the London branch of the Menzies Foundation which sold it for a very good price.

After my mother died, we found amongst her papers – muddled up with recipes cut out from magazines – a small drawing done by my father when he was a schoolboy.

Cricket

My father himself has written about cricket. It was forever one of the joys of his life.

He planted a willow tree in the back garden of our house in Kew, with the eccentric idea that it could, in due course, be chopped down and made into cricket bats. My brother Ken played cricket, and apparently my brother Ian showed promise as a left-arm bowler. Distraught is the best word to describe Dad's reaction when he heard that a schoolmaster had wrecked things by making Ian bowl with his right hand. Later, Ian's eyesight became too poor for him to play cricket at all.

I was a great disappointment because I had and have no real interest in cricket. As I pointed out to Dad, and he conceded my point, he had never taken me to a match or explained it to me. (I was, after all, a girl!) But God bless my daughters who more than made up for me. They understood the game and filled his heart with gladness when they joined him watching cricket on television.

In one of her first games at school our daughter Penny managed to hit five fours and a six. Her older sister, Edwina, reported that she was carried shoulder high off the field. When I said I didn't know she could play cricket, Edwina said, 'No, neither did anyone else.' It soon became clear that she could just as easily be bowled out for a duck. Penny now says that her sports teacher, Miss Brown, would close her eyes when she went in to bat because she couldn't bear to watch the style-less and erratic batsman.

In spite of that, Penny was in the team to play against the male naval cadets at Jervis Bay. When she bowled out two of them in a row, Miss Brown said, 'If you bowl three people out, it's called a hat trick.' She did.

Penny's success was not entirely welcome, however, because the boys were so displeased at being beaten that they wouldn't dance with the winning team that night.

While living at The Lodge, my father dreamt up the idea of creating his own cricket eleven, and spent happy hours working out who to put in his team. He often went to the nearby Manuka Oval and had a pretty good idea of the local talent. Thus, in 1951, when the Prime Minister's XI was initiated with a one day match against the visiting team from the West Indies, my father's side included both Don Bradman and a young Canberran, Bobby Bellchambers.

Jack Fingleton, that great cricketer, was an umpire in the match. He called someone out for a duck. Horrors! That was not in the spirit of *this* game. I can remember Dad admonishing Jack and saying it must not happen again – couldn't he just say 'no ball'?

My father loved those matches, and the associated festivities, not least the dinner at The Lodge afterwards. A long table was set up in the entrance hall, although even then there was not enough room for the entire team.

One night my mother and I abandoned the revelry and went to bed. I was asleep when suddenly the light went on. There was Lindsay Hassett staggering in with the huge bowl of flowers which my mother had arranged on the landing of the stairs. He put it on my dressing table – surprisingly neither he nor the dressing table collapsed under the weight – kissed me on the forehead, and walked out.

The next morning at breakfast – there were a few overnight guests – that same gentleman peered across the table at my father and said, 'Sir, your eye looks a little bloodshot. I think it needs a drop of Murene.' He then got up and walked behind my father, tipped his head back, and put a couple of drops in his eye. This charade was repeated several times.

Did Lindsay have shares in Murene? Would anyone else have got away with it?

There were some who suspected that my father somehow wangled the annual prime ministers' conferences to be held in London at the same time as the cricket season. (Had he been the one organising those conferences that would probably have been true.) Those old celebrities Plum Warner and Gubby Allen were always urging him to go to Lord's and watch a match from one of their boxes, but of course work came first, and he could only take advantage of the offer at weekends.

Football

Australian Rules was a winter obsession. Before my father's prime ministerial years, he spent Saturday afternoon, more often than not, at the 'footy'. Accompanied by Ken or Syd or Syd's son John or other like-minded fanatics, he would buy a bag of peanuts in the shell and munch the day away.

'His' team was Carlton, which recognised his devotion by making him its Number One Ticket Holder. After his stroke, when he was unable to walk easily, they made a sort of sedan chair and a couple of strong men would carry him up to the stand.

Perhaps it is worth mentioning that one of his frequent companions at both the football and the cricket was his opposite number in the political world, Arthur Calwell.

Tennis

My parents were keen tennis players when they were young and belonged to the same tennis club before they were married. As children we were encouraged to play, to the extent that they had a court built at our holiday house, Illira, at Mount Macedon.

The first left-hander to win Wimbledon, Norman Brookes, and his redoubtable wife, Mabel, were friends, so inevitably my parents got to know other tennis players. When Dame Mabel wrote her *Memoirs*, she dedicated the book 'To Robert Gordon Menzies, the best of all of them'.

My parents were often amongst the enthusiastic crowds at Davis Cup matches and got to know many of the players. In London they always did their best to find an excuse to 'escape' and go to Wimbledon.

Vic Seixas was a top American player during the 1950s. I just wish I could find the inevitable verse my father wrote about him that started, 'Good gracious, said Seixas . . .'

Horse Racing

Racing was a different matter: my father was not interested. But during the 1940s his two secretaries, Lennie and Wilkie, were passionate about it. They loved placing bets, often for the flimsiest of reasons: 'Going past in the tram I saw a shop called X, and there is a jockey called X, so I backed his horse . . .'

In the early days of my father's time in Canberra, flying was by no means commonplace, and members of parliament and their staff travelled by train. Inevitably there was plenty of racing talk in the compartments, so although he was not a great follower of that sport, my father got to know a lot of the names of horses and jockeys. Lennie backed the jockey Scobie Breasley, while Wilkie was a fan of Harold Badger.

Travelling between Canberra and Melbourne all passengers had to change trains at Albury because of the different rail gauges. At six a.m. there would be a veritable stampede along the platform as cold and hungry passengers tried to bag seats for the first sitting of breakfast in the next train.

One morning, Lennie was charging along the platform, while Wilkie followed at a more leisurely pace. My father was heard to comment: 'There goes Lennie, Breasleying along in front with Wilkie Badgering her from behind.'

Although he claimed to have no interest in racing, he was actually interested in all sports. Each Saturday in Melbourne he was one of the first to buy the *Herald* (or was it the *Sporting Globe*?) for the sporting results. He would run his finger down the page, and, with his photographic mind, remember all the results.

Occasionally he was invited to a big race. Occasionally he even went. But when he was spotted with his back to the main race – deep in conversation no doubt – he was invited no more.

After having a stroke my father was at the Mount Royal Rehabilitation Hospital in Melbourne. With the wireless next to him he acquired a taste for listening to the races on Saturday afternoons. The legend is that the volume went up and up but the other patients weren't game to complain. With increased interest, he acquired more knowledge and decided – perhaps with Lennie and Wilkie in mind – that he should follow jockeys rather than horses. The most successful jockey at that time was Roy Higgins, so naturally my father took a great interest in him.

My brother Ken decided to give our father a surprise present, and arranged for Roy Higgins to go and see him in hospital. Roy – feeling rather nervous – was met by the matron, who explained that Sir Robert didn't know who was coming to see him, and that he mustn't stay too long. They then walked into the room, and Matron introduced him as 'Roy Higgins, the young man you've been listening to'.

My father's response was: 'Ah, you are the boy from the Riverina.' Then: 'If I don't talk about politics and you don't talk about races, we should get on beautifully together.' And indeed they did. They talked happily for over half an hour, and found they had much in common. Roy said he advised the young jockeys to stay calm, to smile and wave rather than to react angrily when the crowd jeered them if they rode poorly or were beaten. 'They are the paying public, your bread and butter.' The politician could relate to that, all right.

Some years later Roy had a sort of dream, and imagined a dinner party he would like to give. He invited all the top trainers and jockeys, such as Bart Cummings and Tommy Smith and Colin Hayes and Scobie Breasley – *and* Bob Menzies. He wanted to prove to his disbelieving racing colleagues that he really had met the man he admired and liked enormously. Which doesn't necessarily mean politically, because Roy is not political.

That great jockey, Roy Higgins, won 2300 races.

Camera

In the late 1930s my father's friend George Nicholas gave him a movie camera. It was the latest model and the colour film was in a magazine rather than having to be threaded through. This meant that my not very dextrous father could replace the film quite easily. He studied the book and learnt how to use the light meter and practised on the family.

In 1941 he took the camera when he went to London. He was proud of the films he took then, and when he came home he went in to Kodak, they did some editing, and then he showed them off on every possible occasion. After that they were rather forgotten until, after his death, we gave them to the National Film and Sound Archive (NFSA).

Those wartime films are of particular interest, not only because of their images of burning buildings and bomb sites and well known people in the UK at the time, but also because there are very few films of the war in colour.

The ABC found out about their existence and used some footage. The word spread. As the copyright holder, I began to be asked for permission to use segments of the films. I just said yes. Then one memorable day I got a fax from an American television company asking what the copyright fees were. *What?!*

The first person I consulted said, 'We get charged $30 a second for everything we get.'

That must be wrong, I thought.

I rang the NFSA and was put through to a man who immediately became my best friend. He explained that, as I held the copyright, I could indeed charge fees for the films' use: $30 per second was the usual rate, but in some cases $80 was more appropriate. When I expressed horror and amazement, he said, 'It's built in to the production companies' costs, and if *you* don't claim it *they'll* just pocket it.'

My father on Gordon Rolph's boat.

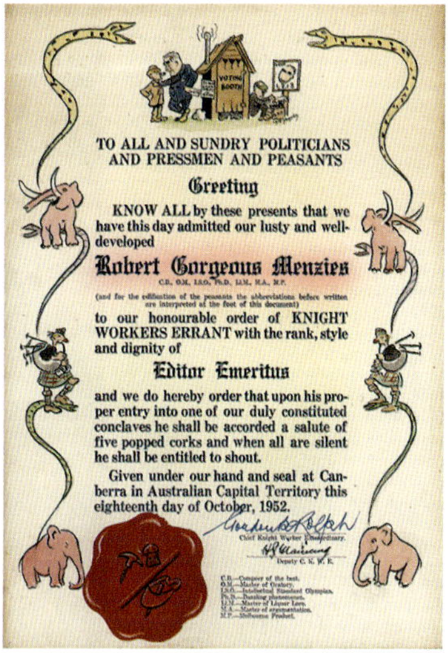

TO ALL AND SUNDRY POLITICIANS
AND PRESSMEN AND PEASANTS

Greeting

KNOW ALL by these presents that we have this day admitted our lusty and well-developed

Robert Gorgeous Menzies

C.B., O.M., I.S.O., Ph.D., LL.M., M.A., M.P.

(and for the edification of the peasants the abbreviations before written are interpreted at the foot of this document)

to our honourable order of KNIGHT WORKERS ERRANT with the rank, style and dignity of

Editor Emeritus

and we do hereby order that upon his proper entry into one of our duly constituted conclaves he shall be accorded a salute of five popped corks and when all are silent he shall be entitled to shout.

Given under our hand and seal at Canberra in Australian Capital Territory this eighteenth day of October, 1952.

Deputy C. K. W. E.

Certificate presented to my father at the dinner given in his honour by the Press.

Blurry but irresistable. My father blowing up paddling pool at The Lodge.

My father with Mary Martin.

My mother and father with Danny Kaye.

Hazel Craig and Ray Maley at Kirribilli House.

Hazel Craig, my brother Ken, Jack and Peg Bunting.

Dad relaxing on a plane.

My parents filming from their plane during a tour of North Queensland, June 1958.

My favourite photo of the Lord Warden of the Cinque Ports.

Mama

The cartoon my mother was so proud of.

Bridge grafitti 'Out Menzies Warmonger', Morwell, Victoria.

Mama multi-tasking: great-grandson Woody and dog Imelda.

Peter, Heather, Sibby, Trini, Penny and Edwina, 1990.

Mama and me at Liberal Party conference in Albury, August 1995.

When I had recovered from the shock I sent back a fax to that television company which, apparently without flinching, replied immediately and accepted my rates.

In the course of making a documentary, *Queen and Country*, for the BBC, William Shawcross came to Australia. He told me he was aware of the Menzies home movies and would particularly like to use the footage my father had taken of the Queen at a picnic. Of course I knew about that segment, but had always said I could not release it as I didn't think it was appropriate to make it public. He urged me to have a rethink, and was so persuasive that I spoke to the NFSA. They were fed up with telling people they couldn't use that bit, and so were only too happy to make a copy for me to send to Buckingham Palace.

Not long afterwards, in January 2000, I received a letter from the Queen's lady-in-waiting:

> I have been watching [the footage] with the Queen and Prince Philip. We were all fascinated to see it and it was great fun trying to identify the other people (and the dogs!) and taking a trip down memory lane. As you say, it was taken when your parents must have been staying at Balmoral. The house on the estate where they were all obviously having a picnic, is a house that was built by

> Queen Victoria and where she used to stay when The Prince Consort was stalking at that end of the estate.
>
> It is about eight to ten miles away from the Castle, up a private road and is now too remote for anyone to live in. The house, which is called Glassallt Shiel (Glassallt being the name of the little stream and Shiel meaning shelter) was built on the shores of Loch Muick (pronounced Mick).
>
> Although Queen Victoria didn't own the land there she did own the sporting rights and when years later the land became available, the late King bought it, which is the significance of those two dates you see over the door of the house. The first man you see in the film is Denys Dawnay who was an old friend of Her Majesty's and Prince Philip's and is sadly now dead. The second man you see is Edward Ford, later Sir Edward Ford. He is over ninety now but in good health and very much on the ball! Both Her Majesty and His Royal Highness were delighted to see the film and have absolutely no objection to your lifting the embargo on it.

In 2006 the NFSA had a large public showing of a selection of films from their archives. The Menzies films received great applause. How delighted my father would have been.

And how appropriate that by February 2013, the copyright fees from all those films had raised $90,183 for the Menzies Foundation.

My father's camera is now held at the National Museum.

Walking and Holidays

In the 1930s my parents bought a house at Mount Macedon. For my father and my brothers and me, plus numerous friends and cousins, it was a great place for holidays. For my mother, it must have been plain hard work. Maybe she needed to brush up her delegating skills. (Do I hear my children saying something about pots and kettles?)

I think it was at Macedon that Ian found his real inspiration to live and work in the country. After school he went on to Dookie Agricultural College, where he ended up as dux. Later he lived in northern Victoria. The people where he settled appreciated his skills, which he shared, and his friendship. Although he died in 1973 at the age of only fifty, he is still remembered there with affection.

At Macedon we cooked chestnuts in the fire and played Monopoly and darts and ping pong, and there was great excitement when the tennis court was built. My father's main recreation was walking. He would stride off, sometimes alone, sometimes with others, and go for miles and hours. My mother would take a car full of young ones and we'd meet him for a chop picnic – a barbecue, in modern terms. I remember that she was thrilled with the discovery that you could cook chops with just a piece of newspaper in a kerosene tin – the fat dripping down kept the flames going.

I am told that I was clutching an armful of naked dolls when we were evacuated from Macedon during the 1939 bushfires. I remember that Parker (Ian) had a burn hole in his blue shirt; he regarded it as a badge of honour and refused to let Mum mend it. The house survived, but was later burnt to the ground in somewhat suspicious circumstances. My parents were so devastated that they just sold the place. That was one of their hopeless real-estate decisions. I sometimes wonder if they would have done better if they had joined us playing Monopoly.

The great sadness for my father was that it was the end of a perfect holiday destination.

To the rescue came Gordon Rolph, who, incidentally, ran the *Launceston Examiner*. He invited my father to go to Tasmania and join him and his family at their holiday house at Low Head on the Tamar River, and go fishing.

Well, that became a place of real relaxation for my father, and he went often. He was fond of the whole family and they were indulgent about his lack of fishing skills. He would sit on the boat, maybe reading or talking or holding a line, with the bait attached by Gordon. Every now and then he pulled up a fish and no doubt said something like 'I think this needs attention.' (Those were precisely the words he used later when handing back to me a damp baby.)

More alarming was spearing flounder. My father climbed into a small dinghy and was pushed off in shallow water, armed with a light and a spear. Every time he saw a flounder and made a stab at it with the spear, the light went off and the boat wobbled and the fish safely swam away. I wish someone had been there with my father's movie camera.

My father thought the Rolphs served the best sausages in the world, and he always came home with a few. Fifty years later their daughter Agnes Humphreys met Peter and me at Launceston Airport with a parcel of sausages from the same butcher, just for old times' sake.

And on the subject of sausages:

One morning in Melbourne my father visited the noted butcher and businessman Sir William Angliss in his office. At eleven a.m. his secretary came in with a sausage on a plate. Sir William ate it, with concentration, then told my father that he tasted one every day to make sure the standard was being maintained.

And on the subject of Sir William Angliss:

On his eightieth birthday Sir William made a speech during which he said, in effect: 'When I was a boy we walked four miles to church and stood and sang "Work for the Night is Coming". Now the young men, if they go to church at all, drive there in their sports cars and sit and sing "Art Thou Weary, Art Thou Languid?".'

Back to Gordon. When he died in 1959, my father wrote: 'I realise more and more what a change was brought about by Gordon Rolph's death.' My father had lost a real friend, as well as a haven where he could truly relax.

Some time after Gordon's death the Chief of the Navy, Admiral Sir John Collins, suggested that my father should go out on the flagship of the navy and have a real holiday away from phones and the pressure of work. My father accepted the invitation with enthusiasm. After my father died in 1978, Vice-Admiral Sir David Stevenson, A.C., K.B.E., wrote to my mother, describing his memories of that time:

> . . . a three week holiday in HMAS AUSTRALIA in the Barrier Reef, when for once he could sit in the sun in a deck chair and rest. We were so proud to have him with us. He did two typical things on that short cruise. He talked to 600 young sailors about tradition, and not only held them spellbound for half an hour, but had them cheering their heads off when he finished. And

that same evening he was dined in the wardroom, and in his farewell speech to the ship, mentioned every officer in rhyming couplets.

My Captain at the time – I was Fleet Navigator – had told me that if ever I were to be promoted, I should be polite to my Prime Minister, and arrive at my destination each time, exactly on time. Sir Robert loved to be on the bridge when, in what we call pilotage waters, the ship had to be manoeuvred with exactness, and when we were coming to an anchorage one day, he stood (with his large frame) exactly where I wanted to peer along a compass bearing. I asked him as politely as possible 'to get the hell out of my way', and the instant response came: 'Can't you see through me Pilot – all my political opponents say they can.' I laughed so much I was thirty seconds late.

In 1975, when Peter and I were in the Philippines, Prime Minister and Mrs Whitlam came on an official visit. One afternoon we were out in a launch on the bay with the President and Mrs Marcos (incidentally, we should have been elsewhere, according to the itinerary). With encouragement, Mrs Whitlam dived in and went off swimming with easy strokes. A couple of security men jumped in after her, but needless to say they had Buckley's chance of getting within cooee of the champion swimmer.

At the other end of the boat, President Marcos was being zipped into a wet suit. He looked at the Prime Minister and asked, 'Aren't you going in?'

Mr Whitlam looked straight at me and said, 'I ask myself, who is the man who was longest in office as Prime Minister of Australia? And the answer is the man who took the least physical exercise. And that's good enough for me.'

I enjoyed that, and some time later repeated it to my cousin Bob Green. Bob didn't smile. 'It makes me mad hearing that sort of thing,' he said. 'I remember, during the war, when I was in the Air Force and stationed at Fairbairn in the ACT. The only warm place was Parliament House, and I often went there to listen to the debates. One night, a note came round from Uncle Bob: "Wait for me afterwards and I'll walk back with you." Well, by the time we got to St John's Church he was in his stride, and talking, and I was panting to keep up. And I was a young man at his fittest.'

Syd's family also well remember Uncle Bob's love of walking. Frequently, he would go for long walks at the weekend, twelve or fourteen miles, and then call (or collapse) in at their house. Syd would revive him with what he called a 'Southerly Buster'. Sadly, none of us could remember the ingredients of that valuable beverage . . .

But to the rescue came someone in the audience one night in 2011, when I was talking about all this. Her name was Margaret Cantor, and she handed me her recipe for a Southerly Buster:

> Equal quantities of BRANDY, GIN, WHISKY, LIME JUICE plus 2 or 3 drops of ANGOSTURA BITTERS. Mix with GINGER ALE. With or without cherry.

I really don't think Syd's version was quite so lethal!

The German philosopher Friedrich Nietzsche wrote: 'All truly great thoughts are conceived by walking.' My father certainly believed that he did his best thinking while walking.

In his earlier days, I think walking or watching cricket or football gave my father his greatest relaxation. During the 1940s, when he was Leader of the Opposition, he regularly used to walk the four miles from our house in Kew to his office in the city. Perhaps he spent some of those hours thinking about the creation of his new party. That was a formidable task. Unfortunately, when he became prime minister, time was his master. All these entertainments could be fitted in only with difficulty.

When my father became PM in 1939 there were people who rushed to be friends. When he went out of office in 1941 they dropped off, only to return in 1949. But no thank you, as my mother said: 'We knew then who our *real* friends were.'

In Melbourne Morris and Dorrie Sallmann were lifelong friends and it didn't matter to them whether my father was in or out of office, or popular, or criticised or loathed publicly. We were always welcome in their house and vice versa.

Just outside Canberra it was Jock and Betty Campbell and their family who provided an escape. I can remember no more entertaining sight than that of my father sitting in a deck chair watching his wife – and others perhaps less pyromaniacally inclined – enthusiastically burning off on their property.

In Sydney the Lloyd Jones were always welcoming and Lady Lloyd Jones (Hannah) was an enthusiastic and unflagging hostess and was always keen to be helpful to my mother.

It's a truism, I suppose, that you can tell what a person is like if you have some idea of their personal interests and activities. For someone like my father, who in one sense was so well known to the wider Australian public, knowledge of the private side can be elusive. So many people had, and still have, what I would describe as a two-dimensional view of him. They would not readily think of him, for instance, as being engaged in the kind of activities I have just described, or of having such a wide range of close personal friendships with people outside politics. His success in the field of politics was due in large measure, I believe, to the balance in his life.

Show Biz

A friend of mine once questioned where young Robert Menzies, my nephew, got his acting ability from, as neither of his parents were actors.

Hullo? (As they say these days.) Just go back one generation and look at his grandparents. Although not officially actors, both Bob and Pat were brilliant in front of an audience.

My first recognition of this, in my father's case, came when I was a schoolgirl. We all went to a play starring the British actor Edwin Styles, and later to a friend's place for supper with some members of the cast. There we had the joy of seeing my father imitating Styles, and 'E.S.' imitating my father.

Over twenty years later, when my father had just been made a Knight of the Thistle, he was speaking in parliament. Jim Fraser, the Labor MP for the ACT, called out, 'You should have got an Oscar, not a Thistle!'

My father enjoyed the theatre and his friends included quite a few actors. In New York he was taken to see a new musical, *South Pacific*, and later went backstage to meet the star, Mary Martin. She explained how she actually *did* 'Wash That Man Right Out of Her Hair' on stage every night, and she invited my father to feel her tightly permed hair. He fell for her immediately. From then on, he never went to New York without seeing Mary in her latest play, or at least speaking to her on the phone.

On one occasion a huge photo appeared on the front pages of the Australian papers. It was of my father flanked by two gorgeous actresses, Mary Martin and Carol Channing. My mother was extremely displeased that she'd been cut out of the picture, and said indignantly, 'I was there too!'

On a later visit there was a strike – actors versus producers. This was no doubt a bit tricky for Mary, because she was an actress and her husband, Richard, was a producer. There could have been no greater indication of Mary's admiration for my father than that she and Richard invited my parents and their entourage to their apartment, where she sang and told the story of her latest play, *The Sound of Music*.

In the early 1950s I travelled overseas with my father because my mother was not well enough to go. In New York an Australian woman, Dorothy Helmrich, who lived there and had strong connections with the theatrical world, asked me if there was anyone my father would like to meet. With thoughts of the record of *The Little Fiddle*, I said, 'Danny Kaye', knowing full well that it was my wish, not his.

To my astonishment – and some horror – Dorothy said she thought she could arrange that, and she did. Danny would arrive at our hotel an hour before we were due to leave for the airport.

Of course, then I had to face the father and explain who Danny Kaye was and what he did. As the appointed hour approached, my father was pacing backwards and forwards muttering, 'Danny Kaye. Never heard of him . . . Danny Kaye. Never heard of him . . .'

I felt slightly sick, very guilty, but thrilled.

There was a knock at the door, and Danny came in and was greeted with civility, of course. He shook hands, walked over to the sideboard and said, 'You aren't going to leave all this behind are you?' and poured himself a drink. He then sat sideways on a chair – legs over the arms – and proceeded to be charming and witty. He and my father immediately clicked and became friends for life.

When Danny came to Australia, he went to The Lodge bearing a priceless gift – one of his trademark hats. Some years later he gave a performance in Melbourne. My parents were in the audience, and my father was in a wheelchair; it was after he had suffered a stroke. In the middle of his act Danny stopped, stepped down from the stage, walked along the aisle and kissed my father on the forehead, then went back and got on with the performance. There was a roar of approval and applause from the audience.

Ralph Richardson and his wife, Meriel Forbes, known as Moo, were a couple my parents exchanged dinners with in London, and with whom they corresponded for years. Noël Coward went to The Lodge, and that association continued. Tommy Trinder, a well known comedian, was a very short man; he wrote on a photo of himself and my father: 'Sorry I am standing in a hole.'

Do musicians count as 'show biz'? Maybe not – but I must mention the cellist Edmund Kurtz. Eddie had married Barbara Bellair, who was at school with my mother, though some years younger. One of his tours included Indonesia, and for that he had a special lightweight suit made in London. Alas, his tailor hadn't really understood what tropical heat was like. After the first half of his first performance Eddie was so dripping that Barbie cut the lining out of the jacket during the interval. From then on, he was cooler but his sleeves were longer, and the buttons on his right sleeve knocked against the cello with every movement of his arm.

From there, Eddie and Barbara flew to Canberra and stayed at The Lodge. My father greeted him with 'A Kurtz upon you!'

In spite of that, Eddie said, 'I will be playing for you, Bob, at the concert tonight.' He gave a great performance.

But possibly my father's greatest bond was with Englishman Alan Herbert, or APH, who was a writer of verse and books and plays and letters to *The Times*, as well as being a Conservative MP. He was a marvellous, eccentric friend. I have a vivid memory of a night in smoggy London when I was with my father. APH and the actress Angela Baddeley dined with us, then we went to the theatre next door. At the end of the performance, as we were leaving our seats, APH suddenly bellowed out, 'Jack! Jack!' Soon we were meeting Sir John Gielgud, who had been in the audience.

It was a dark night and the fog/smog was impenetrable. I suggested that Miss Angela should stay the night in my room, as it had two beds. But no, they both insisted they would travel by underground and all would be well. Alas, even the underground was becoming foggier and foggier, and Miss Angela got home at four a.m., and APH at six a.m.

On my father's seventy-first birthday, APH sent greetings – in verse, of course:

Majestic couple still you fly
Like satellites about the sky
Dear stars, so many wonders done,
Come down at last and have some fun.

He was then quoted as saying: 'I've known Bob for many years. He always sends me a telegram on my birthday – in fact it's always the first to arrive.'

Another poem by Alan Herbert was sung to the tune of 'The Foggy, Foggy Dew' at a dinner party in London after the Suez drama. John Foster Dulles was the US Secretary of State, and he had been less than helpful to my father at that time.

I heard a young man cry in the night,
'I wish I knew what got 'em
To build a great new House for the State
In a swamp called Foggy Bottom.
The mist is on the fields,' he cried,
'The fog is on the news,
Nobody knows where anybody goes,
And I've got the Foggy Bottom Blues.'

'The mist is on the marsh,' he cried,
'The fog rolls down the gullies,

And there's no knowing if I'm coming or going,
For I'm following Foster Dulles.'
(Chorus)

John Foster Dulles, gentle Jack,
Is faithful as a frog:
He lifts his friends upon his back,
And drops them in the bog.
He drops them in the swampy sea,
And while he wipes his shoes
'Oh Lord,' says he, 'what fools these mortals be!'
Which gives me the Foggy Bottom Blues.

'The mist is on the marsh,' he cried,
'The fog rolls down the gullies,
And I can't say where America's today,
For she's following Foster Dulles.'

'Oh gee, that guy is off again!
He's after a new Idea:
But that won't last till the night is past –
He's got idearrhoea.
Ideas, and ideals too –
But I wish he'd take to booze,
For, oh, it's hell what a googygood can do,
And I've got the Foggy Bottom Blues.'

'The mist is on the marsh,' he cried,
'The fog rolls down the gullies,
I steer a course like an epileptic horse,
For I'm following Foster Dulles.'

November 6 is the day of fate
For which we all prepare,
And I can't wait for the golden date –
John Foster won't be there.
John Foster will have put his foot
Too often in the ooze:
No more he'll romp in the Secretary Swamp,
And I won't have the Foggy Bottom Blues.

'The mist is on the marsh,' he cried,
'The fog rolls down the gullies,
And the poor old world to the wilderness is hurled,
No more he'll romp in the Secretary Swamp,
No more he'll romp in the Secretary Swamp,
For it's following Foster Dulles.'

Toby Shaw, my father's London doctor and good friend, added a footnote to this:

> This was rendered full-throatedly and with great gusto, and, as well – surprisingly – nearly all the time in recognisable

> tune, by Bob Menzies after a stag dinner party given by Sir Eric Harrison, the High Commissioner for Australia to speed his Prime Minister on his way – at Stoke Lodge, 45 Hyde Park Gate – on 29.7.57: this the eleventh day after Myles Formby's assault upon his tonsils: testimony enough to M.F.

How I wish that my father could see his grandson Robert giving superb performances on stage today. I can't resist quoting from some of Robert's reviews . . .

As Peer Gynt in 1990:

> Robert Menzies is splendid in the title role . . . it is Robert Menzies's show and as Peer he gives a performance of extraordinary power, virtuosity and emotional range. He begins as a loose-limbed country boy, full of blarney and cheek, only to emerge as a white-suited master of men, all polish and comic glitter.
>
> The penultimate face Menzies proffers, the face of ravaged, uncomprehending experience, is tremendous character acting transcended only by the heroism of what Menzies achieves with the play's very affecting ending. For my money this is the finest performance Melbourne has seen this year. [Peter Craven, in the *Australian*]

In *The Duchess of Malfi* in 2001:

> . . . Robert Menzies, back to his spitting, malicious, awesome best . . . The compelling strength and amazing nuance of the dialogue is clearest when Menzies is speaking, but few others in the cast can match his energy and clarity. [Chris Boyd in the *Herald Sun*]

Later, the same reviewer had this to say:

> Like his grandfather of the same name who was Australia's longest serving prime minister, Robert Menzies has made a living 'standing in big rooms making speeches' . . . he is among the stellar actors of his generation.

And Simon Phillips, then the artistic director of the Melbourne Theatre Company, said simply, 'God, he's brilliant.'

John McCallum, writing in the *Australian* about Samuel Beckett's one man play, *The End*:

> . . . with a performer of the calibre of Robert Menzies the result is magnificent . . . Menzies is superb.

Wouldn't my father, like all of us, be proud?

Yes, He Was a Human Being

It was nearly always people who didn't know my father who referred to him as 'Ming the Merciless' or described him as aloof, intolerant and superior. These criticisms and more have often been levelled against him. Rather than let my bias show too much, I will quote other people.

Letter to the family of the late R.G. Menzies, 12th June 1996

Mr Menzies is rarely portrayed as a man with a 'common touch' so I thought that you might like to hear the following story:

I was a member of the RAAF in Iwakuni Japan during the Korean war. Mr Menzies was to visit Japan and Korea so, of course, we had to have a guard of honour.

About twenty of us 'erks' were lined up on the tarmac and the plane was late. It was snowing . . . suddenly we were dismissed. I asked the officer in charge what has gone wrong? He replied, 'The Prime Minister asked the pilot what the weather was like in Iwakuni. The pilot replied, "Cold and snowing, sir."

'Mr Menzies: "Those boys are doing a great job for Australia and I'm not having them stand in the snow for me. I can do without an honour guard."'

Forty-four years later I still remember this as the decision of not just a great man, but a great man with a concern for others not so great.

Yours faithfully,

Jim Carney

•

My parents went to dinner with old friends in England. Friends, yes, but the hostess was a formidable lady. Their son's twenty-one-year-old bride was terrified at the thought of sitting next to the PM of Australia.

But as they sat down, her neighbour turned to her and said, 'Do tell me, my dear, does your mother-in-law terrify you as much as she terrifies me?' The poor girl relaxed and had a most enjoyable meal, which she has never forgotten.

In fact, my father was an entertaining addition to any dinner party whether he was the host or a guest.

•

Not long after he had arrived in Australia, a Dutch migrant, Max van Apeldoorn, was working in an embassy garden. One day a big black car pulled up and out got a large man who walked over and had a chat: 'Did you have any trouble getting a job?' and so on. When Max found out it was the Prime Minister, he was amazed that he had come to a country where the lack of security made such a thing possible.

•

One night, on his way home, my father put his head round the door of his press secretary's office. He wasn't there, but *his* secretary was busily typing.

'You're working late,' he said. 'Have you had something to eat?'

'No, PM, not yet,' she replied. 'I'll get something later.'

The Prime Minister left and then came back with a tray of food for her.

•

Diana Richardson wrote to me: 'Not many people know about your father's compassion and continuing concern, not only for his friends, but for the children of his friends.' Her father, John Storey (later Sir John), had travelled to the Middle East and Britain with my father in 1940.

Some years later, his daughter decided she was going to marry someone her parents thought was highly unsuitable. They enlisted the help of my father, who went to see them. He then sat down with Diana and spent a long time trying to dissuade her, but to no avail. She married the man and went to live in New York.

Every time my parents went to New York they made sure they saw Diana, and more or less followed the sad saga of her first marriage until it collapsed. Then my father had another heart-to-heart talk with her, along the lines of: 'Well, my girl, what are you going to do now?'

To this day, she is grateful for his support.

•

Here is an extract from a letter to my mother, written by a man who was in the army with my brother Ken at Puckapunyal during the war:

> I feel in these days of vice and corruption it's nice to hear something nice for a change, something that is most

memorable, that is how generous and big hearted was the Hon. R.G.

There was a competition among the State Schools in the Eastern suburbs in the 10 years age group, who could draw the best map of Australia. The final judging was held . . . with a complete wall covered in maps. I was awarded 2nd prize, but the Hon. R.G. disagreed with the judging panel, stating he thought mine was as good as the first, so he gave me a special prize of 2/6. I still have the envelope in which the 2/6 was placed 'special donation from Hon. R.G. Menzies'. My daughter still has the map.

•

Marion, who was an air hostess in the early 1950s, recalled a flight when my father was on board. Amongst the passengers were some young servicemen. They recognised the Prime Minister and asked the hostess to tell him that they would like to buy him a drink. My father said, 'No, I will buy drinks for them.' Marion thought that they'd already had enough and persuaded him to accept their offer. He did. But he then took the drink and sat on the floor in the aisle between them, and chatted for quite a long time. (Were seatbelts not obligatory in those days?)

•

Mario Perrone's father had worked in Alexandria, Egypt, and his family migrated to Australia in 1952. In the 1960s Mario was working for Qantas in Tahiti. His letter to me illustrates my father's ability to listen and remember:

> Your father, then retired, was travelling to the USA via Tahiti. His office sent specific instructions that he did not wish to be met in transit. I was the duty officer in the early hours of that morning, and I did exactly what your father had requested anyone NOT to do! I met him at the foot of the aircraft. He greeted me with: 'Young man, you should be in bed.' I took him to a private office (no lounges in those days) and had a long chat, during which he said to me that the best Italian migrants come from Egypt. A year or so later I saw Sir Robert walking down Collins Street. I went to him and said, 'Hello, Sir Robert, my name is Mario Perrone, we met at the Papetee Airport.' I thought I had made a real gaffe. But I was wrong. With that wonderful smile of his, he replied, 'Of course I remember you. You are the young man from Italian parents who lived in Egypt and was very naughty to meet me in transit.'

•

When Peter and I lived in Manila in 1973 and 1974, I used to help in an unskilled way in the Family Planning Clinic run by Miss Concepcion (yes, that's true). One day a newly arrived American came to assist, and we were introduced. She knew only that I was Australian.

She told me she had just arrived in Manila after living in Melbourne for two years, and we had a general chat about Melbourne. Then: 'One day we went to the football and your Sir Robert Menzies arrived in his car and was driven right round the playing field. The whole crowd stood and cheered. It must be wonderful to be loved as that man is loved.'

These unsought recollections, from a wide range of very different people, mean a great deal to me. Understandably, I hope, I want everyone to know about them.

Stingy with Public Money, Generous with His Own

Making money was never of the faintest interest to my father. He was always personally generous, but public money was another matter entirely. He was adamant that the public purse, the taxpayers' money, should be safeguarded. He was really stingy with public money. It was not to be used lightly or on anything merely of personal benefit to himself. My mother's attitude was exactly the same.

When he travelled overseas he was given an allowance. If he gave an official dinner party but included personal friends he would pay for the whole thing himself. The result was that his allowance was never fully spent. So, after he came home, he handed back to Treasury whatever was left. They were not only surprised but also unsure what pigeonhole to put it in.

Friends Lea and Norman Tanner once drove from Melbourne to stay at The Lodge. When my mother went to take her car out of the garage so the Tanners could put theirs in, Lea said, 'Bob, don't you think it's time you had more than one garage at The Lodge?'

His reply was: 'Lea, I'm the last of the amateurs.'

Actually, my parents had never had more than a single garage, so no doubt it had never occurred to them that another could be handy.

As my father's sole interest in cars was comfort and headroom and good vision, it followed that when he had a car that fitted those requirements he wanted to stick to it. His Commonwealth car drivers were no doubt frustrated and disappointed that he never wanted a new car. He thought it was unnecessary to spend money on a new one. Maybe no one pointed out to him that the old one might turn out to be more expensive in the long run.

Over the years, people have told me stories of my father's generosity. Only recently I had a firsthand account of how, when my father and his small party were travelling by ship to England on an official visit, it came to his notice that the daily allowances for the others were inadequate. So he gave each of them an envelope containing extra money. My informant said it was something they would never forget.

On overseas visits he frequently subsidised members of his official party, particularly the press officers, when, in the course of their duties, they felt obliged to reciprocate the hospitality they had received but lacked the means to do so.

When my father decided to retire, my parents put their minds to where they would live. They had not owned a house for sixteen years and so were 'out of the market'. Happily, they were approached by a spokesman for a group of friends and admirers who were and remain anonymous. The spokesman said, more or less, 'You have done so much for Australia, for us. You've sacrificed your own chance to be well off, so we would like to buy you a house to live in. As you are retiring, this is no bribe.'

(Only recently, I discovered there was a precedent for this: 'In 1945, strapped for ready cash, Churchill considered putting Chartwell on the market after his election defeat. Instead, Camrose [Lord Camrose] arranged for the house to be bought privately by a group of friends and admirers, leased back to Churchill for a nominal rent during his lifetime, and then given to the National Trust.')*

---

* *In Command of History: Churchill Fighting and Writing the Second World War* by David Reynolds, Random House, 2005

My parents were overwhelmed by such generosity and thoughtfulness. After a lot of discussion, they agreed that it would make a huge difference to them, and accepted.

The group said it came with no strings attached, but my parents didn't want that. They decided that, when the money was no longer needed, they would divide it between two schools, my mother's and mine. The schools were not told.

So the house at Haverbrack Avenue, Malvern, was bought. When my father died, my mother sold it and moved to a smaller one. In due course, she sold that and moved to a retirement village in Canberra. She then wrote to tell the two very surprised schools of the donation they were to receive. It all had a happy outcome, and both Fintona and Ruyton used the money to good effect.

My mother handed over the money to the two schools in February 1994, at the headquarters of the Menzies Foundation at Clarendon Terrace in East Melbourne. The Foundation put out a press release explaining in some detail how it had all come about – how the money for a house had been given to the Menzies by a group of anonymous donors, and how it had been used for the purpose for which it had been intended. Now that it was no longer needed, it was being given to the schools, in accordance with my parents' wishes.

The ironic thing was that the media was informed of all this at the same time as one ex-prime minister was building a large waterfront house and another prime minister was buying a big house in Sydney. But the media took little interest in my parents' more modest establishment or the way in which the proceeds of the sale were used. No comparisons were drawn – at least by the media. The headline of the press release was 'MENZIES PROMISE KEPT'. Surely, in the media's view of politicians, that should have been news?!

My father's generosity towards the schools was realised only some years after he had died, and he never had the enjoyment of seeing for himself what a great contribution it was and the pleasure it gave.

What he did see was the pleasure he gave Ken and me when, with generosity on a comparable scale, he used a very large part of the money he had earned from the publication of *Afternoon Light* and *The Measure of the Years* to set up an education fund for his ten grandchildren. Had it not been for the existence of that fund it would have been difficult, if not impossible, for either Ken and Marjorie or Peter and me to meet all those secondary school bills. His own parents had attached enormous importance to education, and so did he.

Irrelevancies

Stay Free

Driving through Gippsland in the 1980s, Peter and I saw some antique graffiti on a railway bridge: 'Out Menzies Warmonger'. It said a lot for the company that made the paint because it must have been at least forty years old.

At the 100th birthday of the Melbourne Scots, in 1994, John Reid said, 'His name was emblazoned everywhere – not by his decree, but by his detractors – on bridges and viaducts: "Pig Iron Bob" was written with grudging respect.'

My father was in opposition when I was in my last years at school at Ruyton, and for some forgotten reason he was on the platform at our Speech Night. Well named. All the girls wriggled through what seemed like interminable speeches by the bishop and chairman and headmistress, so when my father got up to say something his aim was to lighten proceedings with a little joke.

'It has come to my notice that someone has been going round the streets of Kew writing on walls and fences "Stay Free Keep Menzies Out". Now, I understand it was a Ruyton girl who did this, but if the girl who did it will stand up and own up I will give her five shillings for her honesty.'

Well, this was irresistible. I stood up and went up to claim my five shillings. Dad clutched the piano and tears of laughter streamed down his cheeks. The atmosphere had changed to vaudeville. A lot of people there knew I had been going around with a bucket and brush cleaning the graffiti off.

Somehow the story appeared in the paper. Thereby it ceased to be a joke. One anonymous letter I received read: 'Is that the red, white and blue way to play the game? For a little girl to tell a lie for five shillings?'

I was hardly little, and it was a lie, but it WAS fun.

Parlez-vous Français?

At kindergarten my teacher was Miss Snowball, and from the age of six she taught us French. We drew stick figures:

Madame Allumette (meaning 'match') and Monsieur Allumette and their family. My father loved it, and forever afterwards would refer to the Allumettes.

From there, he and I graduated to going to the West Hawthorn Presbyterian Church armed with a French Bible so we could follow the readings in French. Alas, this had no profound effect on my language skills.

When I went to Paris with my parents, my mother, a devoted shopper, wanted to buy some grey gloves. Using our best accents, my father and I tried, '*Est-ce que vous avez des gants gris?*' That produced nothing but a blank stare.

Impatient with us, my mother stepped forward and said in a loud clear voice, 'Have you any grey gloves?'

'Yes, madam.'

Some years later, at a large and grand dinner in India, my father was seated next to the wife of the Russian ambassador. He turned to her with a few friendly words, only to be faced with a gloomy '*Niet*'. Oh dear. Undeterred, he launched into French, but, as in Paris, that failed again. Recognising defeat, he turned his attention to the woman on his other side.

As the evening wore on he became aware that his Russian neighbour appeared to be having a wonderful conversation with the British High Commissioner, seated on her other side. After dinner my father couldn't wait to take that gentleman aside and ask him what language they had in common. The reply: 'None.'

RGM: 'But you were having quite a talk to her.'

HC: 'She says she speaks no English. She speaks no French. I speak no Russian. So I just talk. I recite poetry, nursery rhymes, tell her about my children. Every now and then I laugh – so she laughs too. I've been in this game a long time. If she does understand, that's her problem; if she doesn't, she can't complain that she has been ignored.'

My father was more successful dealing with fellow Australians in French. When my sister-in-law Marjorie wrote to him in French in 1962, he replied:

Ma chere Belle-fille,

J'ai l'honneur d'accuser réception de votre lettre, composée en ce que passe pour Francais (comme nous disons en Anglais), 'et moi de même, avec les bosses'!

Elle m'a donné un très grand enjouement; aussi à ma femme, qui était (ça va sans dire) 'dans le jardin'.

C'est toujours amusant de lire les nouvelles de vos enfants terribles. Dans un façon de parler, leur charme s'augment selon la distance.

Hélas, c'est dommage que beaucoup de personnes de saint (moi, par example) étaient, en jeunesse, si épouvantables!

Acceptez (dans la manière diplomatique) les assurances de ma très haute consideration.

Toujours à toi,

Grandpa

From Geneva to Bangkok

My parents came to Geneva soon after Peter and I moved to live there in 1960. We were renting a furnished house but, allowances being what they were, it was far from luxurious. There was only one chair that we judged to be sturdy enough for my father's bulky frame. Consequently, when he arrived at the house we said firmly, pointing, 'You can sit there.' The next day, accompanied by a very amused man from our office, he went to a store and bought two director's chairs. He refused the offer to deliver them and carried them purposefully out to the car. He wasn't prepared to let them out of his sight.

While he was in Geneva he attended an Australian Heads of Mission meeting. As he was leaving, he turned and surveyed the faces solemnly watching him. 'God rest ye merry, gentlemen,' he said. I understand that proceedings lightened up quite a lot after that.

One night when my father was with us, our Head of Mission and his wife (Bob and Verna Furlonger) invited my father's secretary, Hazel Craig, to dinner. When they asked their four children if they would like to meet the Prime Minister's secretary, three of them said 'Yes!' with enthusiasm. But seven-year-old Tom replied firmly, 'No, I want to meet the Prime Minister.'

Amused by this reaction, Hazel mentioned it to my father, who responded, 'What a discerning young man – I must meet him.' So when my father was leaving, Tom was brought to the VIP room at the airport. My father took him aside to a sofa, where they talked for about ten minutes – the Prime Minister and a seven-year-old.

Later, when asked by his parents what the Prime Minister had said, Tom, who by then was overwhelmed by the occasion, said, 'I can't remember.'

From Geneva, my father went to a South East Asia Treaty Organization conference in Bangkok. He wrote to me from there on 29 March 1961:

> I must have been thinking of you and your next baby when I went to bed, because I dreamed of both of you. It turned out that you had a bouncing son, who, at the time of my dream, was a little under a year old. He was reclining in bed having a conversation with me. You came in beaming. All of a sudden the little baby gave a loud burp. You picked him up and said: 'That's very naughty.'

The baby (remember his age) looked round at me and said quite truculently: 'It's hereditary.'

Fast-forward to 1984. Our daughter Catriona (Trini) had worked in a butcher's shop during her university course, which was Business Studies and Marketing. Having completed that, she couldn't wait to get a 'real' job. Her aim was to work for Shell.

To that end, she applied for two jobs advertised by them, but, although interviewed, she didn't make it. Nevertheless, she referred to herself optimistically as 'Miss Shell' – on the back of envelopes when she wrote to us, for example.

Just at that time I accompanied Peter when he was doing an inspection of several overseas posts. Naturally, my refrain was: 'I wish Trini could get a job before we go . . . I wish Trini could get a job for her birthday . . .'

When we arrived at our last stop, Bangkok, we were met by Chris Lamb from our embassy. I remarked that I had never been there before, and told him about my father's letter written many years earlier. Chris then said, 'I've got a cable for you,' and produced a message from Peter's PA in Canberra: 'Miss Shell has succeeded and starts on Monday.'

Chris: 'Is that the same child?'

Me: 'Yes.'

A Magic Dinner

One night my parents were happily dining with friends, with perhaps eight or ten of them sitting at the table. Their hostess happened to look up, through the door towards the stairs. In a quiet voice she said: 'I'm not sure what this is about, but please, everybody, take no notice.'

Two naked children came in and walked right around the table and out again. The guests dutifully went on talking and eating as if nothing had happened. Shortly afterwards the hostess left to investigate the mystery, and there was much rejoicing when she returned with the answer:

'Mummy, you know that jar on your dressing table? The one called Vanishing Cream? Well we took our clothes off and rubbed it all over us and went into the dining room and walked round and – *nobody saw us*. It really works!'

Health

Physically and mentally robust, my father went through most of his life in good health, although at one time he suffered from a few relatively minor ailments. When he was in London in the early 1950s, he went to see a physician, Dr Cedric (Toby) Shaw, who was chosen on the advice of both Sir James (Jim) McGregor in Sydney and Sir Alec Douglas-Home in London.

Dr Shaw and his wife, Pixie, invited my parents to lunch at their home near Reading, and that was the beginning of a friendship that lasted for life. That friendship has continued down the generations.

Following Dr Shaw's advice, my father had his tonsils removed by a surgeon, Myles Formby. Years later, when Mr Formby died, this notice appeared in a London paper:

> Myles Formby. At Storrington, West Sussex, aged 92. Consultant, Ear, Nose and Throat Departments, University College Hospital 1933–66, and Royal Masonic Hospital 1948–66. President, British Association of Otolaryngologists. Removed tonsils of Robert Menzies (1957) and Ringo Starr (1964).

What a marvellous juxtaposition!

Dr Shaw became a friend not only to my parents, but also to the other members of the Australian delegation which went to London every year. In 1956 my father went to Egypt to try to negotiate with President Nasser. He was accompanied by his secretary and press secretary and the heads of the Prime Minister's Department and External Affairs. Dr Shaw was uneasy about what he perceived to be the dangers to health in Cairo, so, after staying up all night preparing them, he handed over two containers of potions and lotions, labelled as follows:

Box One contained:

Bisadol Tablets
Cascara Tablets

Chlorodyne Tablets
Dicodid Tablets
Dilaudid Tablets
Methedrine Tablets
Phenobarbitone
Seconal Capsules
Salt Tablets
Sulpha Suxidine Tablets
Tetracyn.S.F. Capsules

Box Two contained:

Anthisan Cream
Albucid Ointment
Cetavlon Jelly
Kaolin Powder
Moskitin (anti-insect cream)
Oxo Cubes
Tannafax Jelly
Patch Dressings
Crepe Bandage

The 'boxes' he used were actually old tins which had contained OXO.

Towards the end of his years as prime minister, my father was confined to bed at The Lodge with a bout of flu. He was visited by his doctor, Dr John James, who walked in looking grave. Confronted by such gloom, the patient couldn't resist saying, 'Good-day, digger, did you bring your tape measure?' Dr James wasn't very amused. (The John James Memorial Hospital in Deakin, ACT – now Calvary John James – was named after him.)

Of course, there are always rumours floating around about anyone in the public eye, but, in my experience, they are usually untrue. There was one that stated, quite categorically, that my father had had a colostomy. In 1995 *The Sydney Morning Herald* published an article by Peter Bowers making that claim. I rang Peter, who was extremely apologetic and explained where he got the story, and even followed it up with a very nice letter to me. The paper published my letter:

> In the context of Mr Bowers's article, the paragraph on Sir Robert Menzies is of little consequence. But it is simply not true that he wore a colostomy bag for 30 years.
>
> I understand from Peter Bowers that he went to some pains to check the story, and even had it confirmed by a doctor. That didn't surprise me as I've known of other doctors saying the same thing.

> Before this silly story becomes accepted medical folklore, I would like to say again, publicly (for the third time in 12 months), that the only operation my father ever had was a tonsillectomy – FULL STOP. The nurse who looked after him after he had a stroke said to me, 'He hasn't got a mark on his body.'
>
> He was a pretty awful patient, even with minor illnesses, and I don't think any of us would have survived if he'd had a colostomy.

I suspect the rumour started when he suffered from diverticulitis. That, of course, was less interesting or dramatic for the rumour-mongers.

Peter and I and our children were living in London in the late 1960s when my father had a mild stroke there. When I went to see him in hospital, his speech was slightly impaired. To his relief, he had discovered that if he spoke slowly and carefully, the words came out all right.

'For a Menzies to be deprived of the power of speech is unthinkable,' he said. Even after another, much more serious stroke a few years later, that, happily, never happened. His brain and sense of humour remained intact.

In his last years his nurse, Sister Peters, came to the house. She suited my parents admirably and became a real friend to all of us.

I recall one night Dad was whingeing because the physio was coming next day, and he hated physiotherapy. Sister Peters rebuked him: 'That's a disgrace, Sir Robert.'

He laughed and said, 'You're quite right, dear.'

How much better she coped than a temporary nurse who came in breezily, saying, 'And how are *we* today, Sir Robert?'

His response to that was: 'Not gaga yet, thank God.'

Have-a-look Avenue

My father announced his retirement in January 1966. He believed it was time, that he was past his best and getting tired. Whoever was selected to be his successor needed time to make his mark before the next election.

I have heard it said that he 'anointed' Harold Holt to succeed him as PM, and that he 'anointed' Andrew Peacock to succeed him in the electorate of Kooyong. Not so. They were chosen in the Liberals' normal way, by the parliamentary party and the preselection committee in Kooyong.

My parents moved to their new (second-hand) house in Haverbrack Avenue, Malvern. There had been considerable publicity about the place, and streams of people went past to have a look. My father dubbed it 'Have-a-look Avenue', and so it remained.

After retirement there was no question of stagnating and doing nothing.

My parents had barely settled in Melbourne when they went to the United States for several months.

Bill Battle, a former US Ambassador to Australia, had got to know my parents well, and I suspect he had something to do with the invitation from the University of Virginia to my father to deliver a series of lectures there. However, he was already known to the University, as he had made a speech there in 1963 when he was still Prime Minister. After that, Peter received a letter from his friend Edgar Shannon, who was the President of the University at that time. He wrote:

> The PM gave us a superb address at Monticello, and he and Dame Pattie were memorable visitors to the University of Virginia. No one has ever paid a more warm-hearted and eloquent tribute to the University than the PM did at the dinner at Farmington the evening before his Fourth of July address. It was entirely extemporanious, and all of us are forlorn that we did not have the foresight to arrange for a tape recorder.

Although well aware of the amount of work that would be involved, my father accepted the invitation with enthusiasm, and became a scholar in residence there for several months. It was good for him to have a complete break from his former life.

His first letter to the family after arriving in Charlottesville confirmed to us all what a good idea it had been for him to go there. Following are a few excerpts from that letter:

> Everybody is very kind. We have been taken out to dinner with various people and have in every way been made to feel quite at home. The university grounds and buildings are beyond description. I have seen nothing in the university world to compare with them. The members of the law faculty impress me very much with their keenness and friendliness. They are very serious-minded and anxious to get the best out of their work. The method of teaching is different here but begins to impress me very much. I have agreed to take six seminars on topics within my scope and will therefore before long know what it is to be cross-examined by experts.

While my father was exercising his mind, my mother was coping with a beautiful and fairly large house called Morea, in Charlottesville, and finding her way round the local shops. She felt particularly chastened after she raised her voice in the supermarket: 'Where do I find the Nigger Boy?' (That was the name of a brand of steel wool in Australia.) There were shrieks of horror from Mrs Battle: 'Shh! You can't say that here!'

Both my parents enjoyed the novelty of a white Christmas with both new and old friends.

In 1967 my father was appointed to the historical post of Lord Warden of the Cinque Ports. With his great interest in and knowledge of British history and literature, this came as an enormous honour and thrill for him. He was following men like Curzon and Wellington, and could stay in a modernised and attractive apartment in Walmer Castle, one of five castles built by Henry VIII to defend Britain against the French in the sixteenth century.

He would be expected to wear the appropriate uniform, and his only hesitation about it all was when he heard how much that uniform was going to cost. Not that he couldn't afford it, but 'It will affect your inheritance, dear.' We got over that one quite quickly.

His installation was magnificent, and he wore the uniform that 'went with the job'. I don't think he ever wore it again: he was never one for dressing up. As I mentioned before, even having to wear a white tie – a 'boiled shirt' – sent him into a decline. He was greatly relieved when that went out of fashion.

In fact, the only thing that made us laugh at the miserable time of his death was this bit in the Melbourne *Sun*: 'He loved pomp and ceremony and the trappings of power and position. He loved winged collars with evening dress, striped trousers and black coats . . . uniforms, initials after names, protocol.' Don't believe everything you read in the papers.

Well, the Lord Warden and Dame Pattie were regular inhabitants of Walmer Castle in Kent. In some ways it became a substitute for Kooyong, his electorate. The locals were delighted, and surprised that they saw more of their Australian Lord Warden than they had of his predecessor, Sir Winston Churchill.

My parents got to know a lot of people in Kent, and a favourite form of entertainment was to get them together on the battlements overlooking the English Channel. On one such occasion he was brought down to earth by a voice in the street below, yelling, 'Good on you, Bob!' Australians are great travellers.

When my father died in 1978, his successor as Lord Warden was Queen Elizabeth, the Queen Mother. I can think of nothing that would have pleased him more. My mother, on the other hand, said to me that she thought it was a pity they hadn't chosen someone younger, who could be Lord Warden for longer. How happily wrong she was.

My father gave the castle an Australian painting, which was hung in the private dining room. After his death, I gave the castle a copy of the bust of him by Melburnian Victor Greenhalgh. There are seemingly endless memorabilia of Wellington in the public part of Walmer Castle, and I thought that Menzies should have a presence too. (His successor decided she liked the bust in the private apartments!)

Another post-retirement occupation that gave him immense satisfaction was becoming the Chancellor of Melbourne University. It was 'his' university, which had made such a valuable contribution to his life. He was pleased to be there for sentimental reasons, but also to have the opportunity to give something back. That he did so is clear from the letters my mother received after he died.

From the Chancellor, Sir Oliver Gillard:

> As a graduate and former Chancellor Sir Robert added great lustre to the reputation of this institution. Although his death has deprived us of his wise counsel, the contribution he has made to the University will always be remembered.

The Deputy Chancellor, Professor Emeritus Douglas Wright, wrote:

> Sir Robert had been a great support to the University as a public spirited student and graduate, as a Minister and member of the State Parliament and as a Member and Prime Minister of the Commonwealth Parliament.
>
> His term as Chancellor of this University saw it make its greatest progress. We are greatly indebted to him for the many fine qualities with which he enriched the place. He set a noble standard for the conduct of our business.
>
> His memory is immortal here.

My father went to his office in Collins Street most days. He wrote two books, *Afternoon Light* – some memories of men and events – and *The Measure of the Years*. He always wrote with a lead pencil. Unlike lesser mortals, he made very few corrections and changes. His writing was clear enough not to cause too many headaches for his secretaries.

All of that, plus the usual correspondence and callers and interviews and the odd speech that is the lot of ex-prime ministers, was not what most of us would consider to be 'retirement'.

Happily, he had lots of visitors. His brother Frank was a regular, as was his sister, Belle. She always came armed with a story, often a dramatic embellishment of some of the events in her week, and that gave him a good laugh. That was so important to him.

Former colleagues from parliament, the PM's Department, friends from all parts of his life were always welcome. Anyone who became edgy about staying too long was told: 'Sit down, lad (or lass), I'll tell you when to go.' And he did.

Doug Anthony's relationship with my father remained warm. He was more than just a loyal former colleague: he was a frequent and happily welcomed friend during my father's illness and final years.

Sir Alick Downer, who lived in Adelaide, not only came whenever he was in Melbourne, but also admonished his colleagues in typically biblical fashion: 'We should all be going and sitting at the feet of Gamaliel.'

But the visitor who drew the greatest crowd and gave the soubriquet 'Have-a-look Avenue' real authenticity was Prince Charles, when he called to see my father in 1977.

Mama

When our first daughter, Edwina, was still very young and making experimental sounds and 'words', my mother announced triumphantly that she had said 'mum-R'. 'That's what the children can call me,' she said. Well, that became her name, spelt Mama. My father became Papa, pronounced in the same way.

In the early days of television in Australia, Bob and Dolly Dyer's programme *Pick a Box* was very popular. When Dolly died in 2005, we were struck by the first sentence of an obituary by Mark McGinness: 'After Sir Robert and Dame Pattie Menzies, Bob and Dolly Dyer were probably the most recognised double act in Australia in the 1960s.'

So what about the female half of that Menzies double act?

My mother was born in 1899 in Alexandra, in country Victoria. Not long before that, her aunt, Frances Leckie, died after falling from a horse. Frances was always known as 'Pattie' (why?), so the new baby was named Pattie, with the second name Maie, which was a variation of her mother's name: May Beatrix.

Pattie Maie Leckie was the eldest of three girls. Her sisters were Con and Gwen. They led a happy country life. My mother rode her pony, Comet, to school. She often fell off and had to walk to her 'special' rock so she could climb up again.

In 1978, when my father died, my mother was very touched to receive letters from friends from her early childhood. Violet Anderson wrote: 'I am one of the original Paynes from Alexandra. My father had the store.'

Eve Andrew (Johnson) recalled:

> . . . our school days in Alexandra, the many days I spent at your home, the day when you and Connie dragged me out of the old shaft, and how sad I was when you left there. Bena Bossing at the lolly shop, picnics on the Goulburn River, the egg sandwiches your father used to make for us. Many happy memories we shared.

When Pattie was eleven, her mother died in childbirth and the family moved to Melbourne. Pattie went to school at Fintona as a boarder. One letter recalling those days gives an example of her compassion, even at an early age: 'early days at Fintona – my very first homesick night, you came in and kissed me goodnight'.

For the rest of her life my mother remained grateful to the headmistress of Fintona, Miss Hughston, for the encouragement and education – not only scholastically – that she gave her. In some ways, I suspect, she was a mother substitute.

Pattie spent the holidays with her friends or her father, John Leckie. He was a member of Victoria's Legislative Assembly from 1913 to 1917, when he was elected to the federal parliament as the Member for Indi. Later he became a senator. Sometimes she accompanied him on the campaign trail, so politics was familiar to her from an early age.

She often stayed with her aunt, Janet Leckie, who had a seaside house at Portsea. Fifty years later, she was talking to friends of ours, Freddie and Noela Kiel, who said they had a house at Portsea. After some discussion about exactly where the house was, my mother mentioned the name of her aunt's house: *Terilta*. It was the same house. So when the Kiels asked her to lunch at *Terilta* it was a nostalgic occasion.

Bob, when introduced to Pattie, said, 'You're the girl who used to make eyes at me in church.'

That, possibly, should come under the heading of Family Myths. The story I do believe is that when Bob went to ask Pat's father, John Leckie, if he could marry her, John was pruning his roses. After quite a long time and a lot of roses and inconsequential chat, John went into the house and said to his daughter, 'I do wish Bob would get on with it.'

Senator John Leckie later became a valued member of his son-in-law's cabinet; the two men were on the best of terms.

Pat had two sons, both difficult births, then a stillborn, then a daughter, me, Heather. Her first child, Kenneth Leckie Menzies, was born when she was twenty-one. He was eight weeks early and weighed only three pounds. After two weeks in hospital Pat was sent home with the 'skinned rabbit' – her words – and just had to get on with it. He survived and flourished. That was no doubt thanks to the experience she had looking after her half-brother, John, born when she was seventeen. This might be an indelicate comment, but my mother said she could never eat rabbit again.

Having suffered a lot of adversity, Pat became a woman of steel – not hard, but determined and strong and courageous. These qualities were very much in evidence when her husband became a member of parliament, then a minister, then prime minister.

But nothing in Pat's growing-up years had prepared her for what lay ahead. She had to run the Prime Minister's house, The Lodge, in Canberra. She didn't find that easy because she saw herself as a private, not a general. She very much preferred to do things herself.

She made speeches. At first, it was opening fetes. (Whenever she opened a fete she felt compelled to buy something from every stall; my children were well dressed in 'fete clothes' for many years.) As president of the Auxiliaries of the Women's Hospital in Melbourne, she made many speeches. Later she spoke to groups, mostly women, all round Australia. She continued to speak publicly, and most effectively, for the rest of her life.

On one occasion she was speaking to a large audience in Tasmania, and was distracted and unnerved by a woman in the front row who glared at her throughout, in what seemed a disapproving way. What relief – and amazement – she felt when that woman rushed up at the end and said, 'That was wonderful!'

My brother Ken was in the army during the war. My mother decided to get the mothers and wives and fiancées of his regiment together, and they formed the 2/8th Armoured Regiment Auxiliary. I remember those women having meetings in our dining room, organising fetes and raffle tickets, and packing up cakes and other goodies to send to the boys when they were in New Guinea and Bougainville. Almost more important was the great bond that was formed between those women, and the support they gave each other. Many years later my mother received a letter from a woman who said she would never forget my mother's thoughtfulness in finding out where she lived and going to see her when her fiance was reported missing.

When they were stationed at Puckapunyal, the 'boys' came down to Melbourne whenever they could. One night after a visit my mother got a phone call from Ken, in a panic, saying they had missed the train back to camp. So, naturally, she got into the car and picked them up. She then drove all the way to 'Pucka' with a car full of men, and with a couple more soldiers on the running boards. (Remember them?) They managed to avoid being AWL (absent without leave).

Tony White, the son of one of my brother's fellow soldiers, wrote in 2007:

> I had the privilege of personally meeting Dame Pattie when at the request of the 2/8th my wife and I hosted some four years of the annual church service at our home. She was in her early nineties, super embracing, a spark who engaged all around her with no bullshit, airs and graces. When she arrived 'her boys' would form an entrance aisle to welcome this loved friend of theirs.

In 2007 the 2/8th Armoured Regiment Auxiliary was, sadly, disbanded. In their final publication Val Jackson, one of the stalwart wives, wrote:

> Dame Pattie as President of our day and night meetings with wives and sweethearts during the war was an inspiration. Later the 2/8th Association was honoured by her Patronage. Dame Pattie enjoyed every minute with 'the boys and girls' as she said in her last speech to us.

When my father was prime minister from 1949 to 1966 my mother was more than fully occupied. One of her 'jobs' was to receive calls from the wives of foreign heads of mission. She was soon on good personal terms with them, and they trusted her and confided in her. One wept on her shoulder because her husband was having an affair with an Australian woman; another had a husband who beat her.

Thessa, the young wife of a Chargé d'Affaires had her first baby in Canberra, and became quite desperate about how to handle such a tiny creature, in a new country and far away from any support she could have depended on at home. She asked, 'Dame Pattie, will you please replace my Mum?' I suspect that suggestion was accepted with alacrity: my mother showed her how to change nappies, helped with the feeding and generally provided support which has never been forgotten. My mother was far from being a remote and grand Public Figure.

Because I was living at The Lodge for several years before I was married, my parents got to know a lot of people of my generation. My mother was hospitable and very considerate of the young, and enjoyed their company. Some were foreign junior diplomats, and in later years those who returned in more senior roles remarked that they'd had greater access to the Prime Minister when they were Second or Third Secretaries than they had later as Ambassadors.

One day, friends of ours invited some people to come for a drink to meet their new baby, but a black car drove up and out jumped my mother, who walked over and said, 'I thought I could take the nappies and wash them for you.'

My friend said she had done them and they were on the line. Not deterred, my mother offered to wash up.

'No, no, no, *please* don't!' The poor young mother was horrified at the thought of the PM's wife washing up while her friends were enjoying a party.

Eventually persuaded, my mother gave in, but before leaving she opened the boot of the car and produced a basket of cutlets, complete with paper frills, and vegetables from the garden all ready to cook.

An Indian High Commissioner, General Cariappa,

brought his niece Sagarie to act as his hostess. Many years later, she wrote to me:

> Your mother's incredible gift of remaining so down to earth and normal despite the highest office your father held, I knew only too well as a twenty-year-old college girl. I never dreaded meals at The Lodge as I did at the other diplomatic do's. Your parents were always so kind and caring and human. I was never awed by them. It's all so clear after forty years.

Travelling became a constant part of my mother's life. A semi-packed suitcase had a permanent place as part of the furniture in the bedroom. Also at the ready was what became known as the 'Red Box'. It was really a cosmetic case and contained lotions and potions and safety pins and bandaids and jewellery – everything, really. It was conceded to be the most valuable object amongst all the luggage of the entire delegation when travelling overseas. 'Where's the Red Box? . . . Who's got the Red Box?' were often-repeated questions. The Queen's Red Box could not possibly have been more treasured.

Once settled on a plane, my mother happily went on with her tapestry. She was never at a loss with plane delays or broken down cars: out came the tapestry.

My mother's first journey overseas was in 1935, when my father went to London to appear before the Privy Council. The trip had two royal highlights for her. One was being presented at court. In the haze of excitement and nerves, all she could recall was that, as she rose from curtseying to Queen Mary, the Queen asked, 'What is the most magnificent thing you have seen since you came to London?'

Pat: 'You, Your Majesty.'

From there to call on the Duchess of York and her two young daughters, Princess Elizabeth and Princess Margaret Rose. They gave Pat a photo signed by each of them. My parents gave them a photo, presumably of my brothers and me. My mother explained that I had lost my front teeth, so the photographer had painted them in. Apparently, Princess Margaret Rose was fascinated and wanted to know why my teeth had fallen out.

I hope it is not disrespectful or presumptuous to say that was the beginning of a long and warm association with that family.

A few years later, when my father was Attorney-General, my parents were in London at a large and formal dinner, with our Prime Minister Mr Lyons. At one stage my mother went to the ladies' room, walking in just as Mrs Lyons (later Dame Enid) walked out. My mother was astonished to hear the two attendants saying, 'How amazing for a woman like that to be living in that primitive country.'

In icy tones, my mother said, 'I am Australian too. There are lots of people like us there.'

On a visit to South Africa in the early 1950s my mother was regularly interviewed by the press. A frequent question was: 'Mrs Menzies, is it true that you can cook?'

Slightly irritated, in the end she said, 'I am Australian. If I could *not* cook, *that* would be news.'

At the time of the coronation of Queen Elizabeth II, in 1953, there were lots of crowds and parties and celebrations in London. At one big gathering my mother, who was tiny, was standing next to Queen Salote of Tonga, who was not. Plates of food – sandwiches, sticky buns, cakes – were taken round. Every time they were offered, the Queen took one. After many little goodies had been consumed, she finally said, 'No, thank you.' She turned to my mother and added 'I'm on a diet, you know.'

Arriving in Delhi, my parents, with me in tow, were taken to stay at the President's palace. My parents were shown to a suite of rooms, while I was taken to another room that seemed like a hundred yards away. My mother was horrified and declared that she wasn't going to have me so far from them – even though I *was* an adult! So I was installed in their dressing room. Well, the poor servants; they didn't know how to cope with such odd people. They followed their normal routine and insisted on helping my father dress for dinner. My mother ended up getting dressed in a cupboard.

On yet another stay at some grand house or palace overseas (thank goodness The Lodge is not on that scale), a maid took my mother's dress to iron it. It didn't come back in time for dinner, so in desperation she wore another one. When she returned to the room after dinner there was the original dress draped splendidly on the bed, but with all its permanent pleats ironed out. Quite a feat – but rather distressing.

Another dress drama was self-inflicted. I was staying at The Lodge and my mother was dressed and ready to go to Government House for dinner. My baby cried and I went to pick her up, but her determined grandmother got there first and picked up the child, who was promptly sick all over the sequins on the beautiful taffeta dress. Quite undaunted, my mother changed and put the vomit-laden garment in a bath of cold water. Miraculously, that dress lived to see another day.

In the days before prime ministers had their own planes for overseas travel, there was nothing exclusive about the travel itself; all the grandeur was on and after arrival. In fact, on one flight back to Australia the trip became the very opposite of glamorous. A young couple with a baby staggered on, looking exhausted. The baby had cried for hours on an earlier leg of their journey, and it continued.

Eventually my mother, with her extraordinary weakness for babies, even wet and screaming strangers, said, 'Give the child to me.' The parents collapsed and went to sleep, while she walked up and down the aisle, nursing it. She calmed the poor little thing down, then sat with the sleeping, sodden bundle in her arms for two hours, cautious about moving in case he woke up.

We discovered later who the grateful parents were. The baby became the Official Secretary at Government House in Canberra.

In Britain in 1941, my father went to the factory where Humbers – which happened to suit his requirements, with comfort, headroom, good vision, etc. – were made, and met Billy Rootes (later Sir William) who ran it. The happy outcome was that my father bought a Humber which was sent to Australia. It remained our family car for many years, with a gas producer on the back during the war. My mother became an expert at coasting down hills, and anything else that would conserve petrol. My brothers and I all learnt to drive in it. My father, as far as I recall, drove it only once. Maybe that's another example of Pat's attitude that all domestic and practical matters were better left to her.

She was practical with the telephone, too. My parents never had a silent number, and were, alas, always available to anyone. Inevitably there were crank calls, even in the middle of the night. After their retirement to Melbourne there was one particularly persistent midnight caller. The police were alerted, but only once was the perpetrator nearly caught. He/she had rushed away from a public phone and left the receiver dangling. My mother took matters into her own hands and bought a whistle, which she blew into the receiver. That solved the problem, but also, no doubt, wrecked someone's hearing.

A far cry from the Humber was the small and feeble car that my mother bought when they lived in Melbourne after my father retired. It sounded like a sewing machine. An old sewing machine. After driving a manual car all her life she found it difficult to adjust to an automatic. She didn't really trust it. So at all times when her right foot was on the accelerator, her left foot was on the brake. It was noticeable that the brake light was always on, and indeed the brakes had to be relined three times.

I mustn't be mean, however: she was actually a very competent driver. Peter and I were her passengers one day, and as we left my brother's house she hit something in the middle of the driveway and knocked off the muffler. We caused quite a stir as we roared home, with people turning to abuse 'these dreadful hoons', only to see a dear little old lady at the wheel.

One day, when I arrived to visit, my mother said, 'Heather, now you're here with your car, will you follow me to the garage? I need to leave the car there because the front doors won't open from the inside.'

H: 'So what have you been doing? Were you calling someone over to open it for you?'

Mama: 'Heavens, no. I just climb over the back of the seat and get out the back door.'

H: 'Mother, you can't *do* that!' (She was well over eighty at the time.)

Mama: 'And how else would you expect me to get out?' (in squashing tones.)

She beat me to the garage by a few minutes, and by the time I got there she was out of the car, having used her own method.

In Melbourne, the possums that damaged her much loved garden aroused her ire. She borrowed a possum trap, and, nothing daunted, climbed a ladder and managed to heave it onto the garage roof. I think she caught about four in two or three nights. She was particularly proud of a mother and baby, so she drove them, in the trap, in that feeble little car, to show them to her young granddaughter Elizabeth (our daughter, known to us as Sibby), in Geelong. She finally released them near a river far from Kooyong where she lived.

Another animal encounter that was a bit more alarming occurred when she was staying at Chateau Tahbilk, her favourite vineyard, with her great friends Eric and Mary Purbrick. After dinner at the cellars, she walked through the garden and back to the house. Once in her room, getting ready for bed, she became aware of a strange noise in the corner. She kept putting her foot on the floor, thinking there must be a creaky floorboard. But as she looked again at the collection of walking sticks standing there, it dawned on her that the noise was coming from a small snake coiled up amongst them. Pretty rapidly, she went out into the passage and called out, 'There's a snake in my room!'

Her dinner companions were just returning in high spirits. 'Ha, ha, ha – Pat's got a snake in her room!' To their astonishment it was true, but they gathered their courage and rescued the lady in distress from the monster. It was a mere baby, not much more than a foot long.

It was only then she recalled that when she had come into her room, in the dark, and reached for the light switch, she had felt something on her shoulder. She'd brushed it off, but then she remembered she had heard something land on the floor. Horrors! It wasn't an innocent piece of greenery from the garden – it was the snake. With pride, she kept the poor dead snake in a jar for years.

That all might give the wrong impression. She did love some animals very much and they loved her. During one of our postings in Canberra we inherited a third-hand nondescript dog called Jaffa. He decided he belonged to us, and became very protective. One morning I fed the baby, Sibby, and left her asleep in the pram under a tree, with Jaffa nearby, and Mrs Mitchell in the house. When I got home from shopping my mother was there – why? Apparently Sibby started crying but Jaffa wouldn't let Mrs Mitchell go near *his* baby. He could be quite aggressive. Poor Mrs M. rang my mother, who drove straight round, and, of course, Jaffa allowed her to pick up the baby.

In the 1980s, when we were living in Melbourne, she would never hesitate to look after our pets when we went away. We received a memorable telegram from her the day after we had deposited our cat with her. 'I SLEPT UNDER THE SPARE ROOM BED. THE CAT SLEPT ON MY BED. HOW DID I READ THE PAPER WITH THE CAT ON MY CHEST. LOVE MUM.

Thank heavens she never lost her sense of fun.

After my father's death in 1978, my mother continued to be in the public eye. Happily, she was photogenic. After one Liberal Party function there were huge photos of Dame

Pattie in the papers and on television. The next morning she received a letter addressed to 'Ms P. Menzies' – from, believe it or not, the Liberal Party. She was not amused.

On the other hand, she was not merely amused but thrilled and proud when she was the subject of a cartoon in one of the newspapers. 'In all these years I have never been the subject of a cartoon before,' she said. She was shown sitting in a deck chair, yelling through a megaphone at Mr Keating, who was depicted as a kangaroo. It came about because she had responded fairly crisply to one of Mr Keating's numerous attacks on my father, and on the monarchy.

In 1988 an ABC TV mini-series about the Labor Party, called *The True Believers*, was aired. Inaccurately, it was described as a documentary. The makers' idea of Menzies bore no resemblance to the man anyone knew. In fact, few of the characters were true to life. My mother watched some of it with us, and when we said, 'That's *you*, Mum – quick, look!' her comment was: 'Don't be ridiculous – I've never worn purple in my life.'

A small point indeed, but an illustration of what a pity it was that no one thought even to pick up the phone and ask us a few questions.

In rainy weather my mother would don a rather dreary grey plastic raincoat and an equally unbecoming grey plastic hood over her hair. One wet day she drove to the market in that ensemble and pushed her shopping trolley around, looking anything but a public figure. She waited amongst a rather large group of customers at the fish shop, Claringbolds. She had a sentimental attachment to it because the original Claringbold had been the fishmonger in Kew when she lived there for twenty-five years.

'Yes, love, what would you like?' the shopkeeper asked.

'A small piece of whiting.'

The man held up a small piece, but she said she wanted something even smaller. She handed him a five-dollar note and he gave her a handful of change. When she looked at it, she realised he had given her five dollars in coins. She tried to correct him, but he waved her away: 'That's all right, love.' She was terribly embarrassed, but I think it's one of the nicest things I've heard – a really thoughtful and generous gesture for a little old lady who looked fairly poverty-stricken.

Living alone in Melbourne, my mother had a fall and broke her wrist. She was taken to hospital and her arm was put in plaster up to the elbow. The next morning her breakfast tray was brought in and plonked down, almost out of reach. Having managed to pull it closer, she discovered that the butter was wrapped in a little packet. Aged nearly ninety and with only one hand operative, she decided it was all too hard, so discharged herself.

From Canberra, I was appalled, but Mum said she was much better off at home. 'For breakfast I put a slice of bread in the toaster and some butter on a plate into the oven. Then I drop the toast onto the melted butter and swish it round. And you know that marmalade I made that was rather runny? I pour that on.'

Always a believer that idleness was wicked and anyway boring, she prevailed on someone to put her tapestry onto a frame. A friend threaded several needles in different colours and away she went one-handed, happily occupied.

In 1978 Dr Alan Gregory provided the necessary enthusiasm to the Liberal Club at Monash University giving the students the courage to call on my father to ask if they could name an annual lecture after him. For thirty years Alan was the chairman and leading light of the Sir Robert Menzies Lecture Trust, and it continues to thrive. I don't think my mother ever missed a lecture, and she always took a great interest both in the lectures and in the students who attended them.

An illustration of how well she got on with the young is given by this letter from a man in London: 'When my son took a year out from Oxford and went to work in Australia, he accidentally met Dame Pattie and, at the tender age of 19, fell deeply in love with her!'

Alan was also the inspiration behind a dinner in Melbourne to celebrate my mother's ninetieth birthday. With 750 people there to wish her happy birthday, she kept worrying about what to say. We made calming noises: 'Just say thank you, that'll do.'

When the time came, that tiny figure went to the microphone and spoke vigorously for over thirty minutes about sitting on platforms at public meetings, and ships she had launched. She inspired great audience reaction with plenty of laughs – all without a note. ('Don't be silly, Heather. It's no use having notes. I can't see to read them.') One of those present said, 'I would have travelled for days and sat on concrete to hear that.'

About a year later, she fell down the front steps of her house and suffered bad bruising on her legs and up to her waist. This time she went into a small private hospital, and as she was being installed I went to the office to sort out the admission form. I remarked to the girl filling it in that the space for the date of birth would have to be changed from '19__' because she was born in the last century, in 1899.

A later question was: 'Has she been a patient in this hospital before?'

'Yes,' I told them, 'when her first child was born here, seventy years ago.'

So there was no doubt about her age. In spite of that, she was taken to the shower and left, ninety and damaged, to fend for herself. With difficulty, she managed to get herself back to bed.

The next day while I was there, two nurses came in and put their hands under her bottom and started to lift her. When she complained, loudly, I asked if they knew what was wrong with her. No. When they looked at her bruises they understood her objections only too well. Hospital, as they say, is not for the faint-hearted. (Dear nephews, excellent nurses, I hope you will forgive me for that comment.)

In 1992, aged ninety-three, Pat was invited to the naming of two cricket pavilions at Manuka Oval in Canberra. One was to be named after my father, and the other after another former PM, Mr Hawke. We listened to speeches from the Chief Minister, the President of the Cricket Association, and Mr Hawke. As he spoke, my mother turned to me and whispered, 'I was going to tell that story. Help! What'll I do?'

But she needed no help, of course. She went to the microphone, banged her hand on the lectern, and said, 'You've taken all my stories!' Then she proceeded to tell a better one. I cherish the memory of Mr Hawke's rapt attention, and his look of surprise and admiration.

The only other (sort of) connection we have with Bob Hawke was when our daughter Edwina was driving past

The Lodge with her five-year-old daughter, and said, 'That's where Granny Pat used to live.'

Alice thought for a while and then asked, 'Did Granny Pat used to live with Bob Hawke?'

Three years before she died, my mother went back to Canberra to live, and moved into a self-care unit in a retirement village. She soon made it look and feel like home: she had a talent for that. After all, The Lodge had become very much a Menzies home.

In 1961, when she launched the liner *Canberra*, she had admired the green silk curtains which were part of the furnishings on board; generously, the P&O people gave her a bolt of the material. She kept it until my father retired and then had it made into curtains for the sitting room of their house in Melbourne. Later, when she moved after my father's death, the curtains, altered to fit, moved with her. We then took the curtains to Canberra – leaving her with borrowed ones – and they were altered yet again to fit the new house. The result was that, when she walked in, the place already had a familiar feel.

Back in Canberra, my mother immediately set about creating a garden. Her new neighbour was surprised one morning to hear her barking like a dog. 'Oh, dear, I do hope I didn't disturb you,' she said. 'I was trying to frighten the birds away.' Her method worked, because within a year she was giving away home-grown beans. The downside was that she managed to break a rib while hammering in stakes for the tomatoes.

One day Peter happened to call in. She greeted him accusingly: 'Why didn't you come earlier? I got locked in the courtyard and couldn't get out.' Having protested that he wasn't expected at all, Peter asked her how she had got out.

She had, with an effort, pushed some of her many pots, with plants in them, over to the six-foot-high wall – much taller than she was – and climbed up. Somehow she got on top of the wall and then fell over to the other side. 'You won't tell Heather, will you?' she demanded.

'Of course I will,' Peter replied. 'But why didn't you just climb up enough to put your head over the top and call out to someone going past?'

'You couldn't expect me to stand there all day!'

She had an alarm round her neck but either forgot about that or 'didn't want to be a nuisance', and anyway she was too impatient. And she was, after all, only ninety-five.

When she died at the age of ninety-six, Princess Alexandra wrote: 'I can just see Dame Pattie climbing celestial walls.'

My mother – Mum, Mama, Fred (to my brother Ian/Parker), Pat, Pattie, Dame Pat, Dame Pattie, call her what you will – was a remarkable woman by any standards. Widely regarded as the 'Queen Mother of Australia', she was loved and admired even by people who had never met her.

We were very pleased to read some wonderful obituaries in the papers. But two that appeared in London are worthy of note, for the wrong reasons.

The London *Times*, which had published her birthday every year since 1954, this time gave her the wrong birthday. It then went on to state that 'her mother was a successful journalist who wrote as Hattie Knight'. Hattie was, in fact, her not greatly loved stepmother.

And: 'Her family went to the Presbyterian church in nearby Jeparit, where the Menzies family also worshipped.' There was no Presbyterian church in Jeparit, and Jeparit was nowhere near Alexandra, where my mother was born, nor Melbourne, where she lived from the age of eleven.

London's *Daily Telegraph* was positively controversial: 'William McMahon held her accountable for the distrust with which Sir Robert Menzies viewed him. McMahon believed that Dame Pattie had seen him as a potential match for her daughter, and that she resented his failure to fill the role.'

It's even hard for me to type that without exploding with rage and indignation! To repeat myself: don't believe everything you read in the newspapers.

From the many hundreds of letters I received when my mother died, here are a few of the tributes:

From David Adam: 'Seldom have I seen such unanimous acclaim for a person who lived so much of her life in an arena of political conflict.'

From Dr Lloyd Thomson: 'Not the least remarkable aspect of her life history is that in her widowed years she should have emerged as so revered and recognised a national figure.'

And my favourite, from my friend Carol Clendinnen: 'She was just magic and the world has lost a star.'

These tributes were all private, addressed to me. During her lifetime there was a formal public one: the citation when she was awarded the GBE (Dame Grand Cross of the Order of the British Empire) in 1954. My account would not be complete if I didn't quote it in full:

> In recognition of years of incessant and unselfish performance of public duty, in hospital work, in visiting, addressing, and encouraging many thousands of women in every State of Australia, including very remote areas, and in the distinguished representation of Australia on a number of occasions overseas.

Finale

I've had a lot of fun, and hours of unaccustomed brain work, writing this. I know it's a real hotchpotch of memories and quotes and opinions, but then I've never had an ordered or disciplined mind. It's too late now to change.

My hope is that I have brought my parents to life as real people – not just names on the pages of newspapers or history books – and that you will be able to see for yourselves how right Sir Walter Crocker was when he said to me, 'You are one of fortune's most favoured children.'

If it seems to you like a hagiography, I can only say: 'Of course it is. After all, this is about my beloved parents.'

Acknowledgements

Thank you, Jane Palfreyman, for agreeing to publish this book, apparently without hesitation. And it wasn't just for old times' sake. Was it?

Julian Welch and Laura Mitchell and others in the editing world have devoted many hours of work to every page of this book, and I appreciate their contribution. The task has been made more difficult for all of us by our differing approaches to words and punctuation, no doubt explained by the great difference in our ages, and the usages we have learnt and grown up with. Consequently the result has been a real compromise, and quite an achievement.

John Nethercote has saved me from getting a few names and dates wrong.

Large slabs of this have been written, unwittingly, by others, in the form of letters and articles and remembered words. Whether you are here or in the hereafter, I am extremely grateful for your huge contribution.

My long-suffering family deserve the biggest thanks:

My husband Peter has had inspired thoughts and has jogged my memory over the years this has been brewing. He and Dwina have laboured for hours over edited versions with controversial commas and hyphens added or deleted. Trini and Ellie labelled, wrapped, and delivered photos. Penny kept us in good health. Sibby and her family are always at the ready if we need them; Pip wielded her camera to good effect.

All my family and friends have been supportive in many different ways. They have made lots of helpful suggestions, and I hope they can see that I have taken note of them.

Not family, but near enough, was Hazel Craig. It is a great sadness that she died this year at the age of nearly ninety-nine, so didn't make it to see this published. Her memory was astonishing, and vital for this project.

Another woman, also no longer with us, to whom I am indebted, is Miss Denham, who taught me English at Ruyton. I hope I haven't let her down.

Index